Off in Zora

Also available from Booksellers House

Cody's Books
Fifty Years in My Bookstore
The Haunted Bookshop
A Memory of Vermont
Parnassus on Wheels
Sunwise Turn
Wise Men Fish Here

Off in Zora

A Modern-Day Tale of a Traveling Bookseller

By Alan Armstrong

BOOKSELLERS HOUSE

An Imprint of Booksellers Publishing, Inc.

*A Wholly Owned Subsidiary of
the American Booksellers Association*

BOOKSELLERS HOUSE

An imprint of Booksellers Publishing, Inc.

A wholly owned subsidiary of the
American Booksellers Association
828 South Broadway
Tarrytown, NY 10591
(914) 591-BOOK, (800) 637-0037

Cover Design: Faith Moeckel/FMA Publication Services

ISBN: 1-879923-13-0

First Booksellers House Printing, June 1997

Printed in the United States of America

ACKNOWLEDGMENTS:
p. 23: "In the Poppy Field" by James Stephens. From *Collected Poems,* Macmillan
(London) & Company, Ltd. Copyright © 1954.
p. 28: *The Practical Cogitator* by Charles P. Curtis, Jr., and Ferris Greenslet. Copyright
© 1945. Reprinted by permission of Houghton Mifflin Company.
p. 93: "What Lips My Lips Have Kissed" by Edna St. Vincent Millay. From *Collected
Poems,* HarperCollins Publishers. Copyright © 1923, 1951 by Edna St. Vincent Millay
and Norma Millay Ellis. All rights reserved. Reprinted by permission of Elizabeth
Barnett, literary executor.
p. 131: *Kafka Was the Rage* by Anatole Broyard. Copyright © 1993. Reprinted by
permission of Carol Southern Books.
p. 133: *Images and Shadows* by Iris Origo. Reprinted by permission of John Murray
(Publishers) Ltd.
p. 141: *The Story of Yale University Press* by Clarence Day, Jr. Reprinted by permission
of Yale University Press.

On the Cover: Alan Armstrong and Tom Panzera (holding book) with Zora.

CONTENTS

For my partners, T. P. and Jefe

This gentleman of ours was close on fifty, of robust constitution but with little flesh on his bones and a face that was lean and gaunt. He was noted for his early rising, and on occasion when at leisure, which was most of the year around, he was in habit of reading books in which he became so immersed, spending the whole nights from sundown to sunup and his days from dusk to dawn in his pourings, that finally, from so little sleeping and so much reading, his brain dried up. When his wits were gone beyond repair it appeared to him fitting and necessary, in order to win a greater amount of honor for himself and to serve his country at the same time, to become a knight-errant and roam the world.

—*Don Quixote*
After the Samuel Putnam translation

CHAPTER 1

Off in Zora

We're off in an old VW bus my wife, Martha, loaned me. She's a painter—bought it used to carry paintings, stripped out the seats for space. The title says Zora is a rebuilt wreck. The salvager repainted it in three tones—mahogany below, then dark redwood, and cream on top. Martha put in a rebuilt engine more powerful than the original.

Even loaded down with books the bus moves out like a bloated Porsche, but it wanders, a little this way, a little that, you're never sure. The windshield is dinged and hazed, so scratched that oncoming lights at night don't shine, they glow. The seats are shredding down to the wire frame, little piles of horsehair and jute underneath. Mice got in while it was garaged last winter.

When she's cold Zora is a balky starter. I have to park her on a hill in case I need to kick the engine going. Sometimes we end up dead in Martha's field. That happened this morning in the dark. Martha had to drive down to give me a jump from her battery.

Aboard, a fiftyish man, compact, middle height, slate eyes, graying hair, a laughing, talking mouth, not a bad-looking face all in. And Jefe, a tough little black poodle the size of a flared-up cat. Our daughter left him with me ten years ago when she headed off to college.

Jefe is cut like a terrier and imagines himself huge, lunges snarling at anything that approaches suddenly. I come home and he's at the door wheeling and grinning like a little buffalo, everything forgiven. Most places I go he goes. He gets silly around other dogs that come up slowly, behaves like a dapper, stiff-legged clown at first, sniffs everything he can, then dashes around in circles only a poodle could follow. Out walking at home we often encounter a husky named Max who barks as we approach his yard, then crouches and slithers toward us as we draw close, his waving curled tail giving him away. Jefe yips with excitement at the snake act, goes up gingerly, snaps and cavorts. Max smiles and takes up with us.

"Sell a bunch!" Martha yelled as we ground out at dawn for Franklin. Jefe settled with a happy squeaking sigh of pleasure into his travel box. He's good for two hours or a hundred miles, then he wakes and shakes his dog-tag jewelry, clattering and announcing his intentions in sneezes, half-growls, and songs (there's a lot of music in this dog). His range is about mine, so it works out.

I was eight or nine and stuck in bed when my father, Stuart (that's what we all called him), read me the story of a small, feisty man peddling books from a horse-drawn wagon. This was a living more fun than going off every morning like Stuart did to a desk in a big room with other desks and not being able to go outside when you wanted.

I named my book van Zora after my father's aunt. Zora was big-faced, friendly-looking, not pretty. She wore clothes "to drape," as she put it, and she sold the same, had a southern accent, and for all she was abrupt she laughed a lot. She and her sister Alta sported some fine gold teeth, the gift and advertising of their brother Lacy, dentist in town, who worked with a foot-pedal drill. When we went to visit on family trips we'd line up on Saturday for a year's worth of dentistry. He had his office in his home and kept peacocks in his yard. You could watch them flaunt and parade, hear them scream while he pedaled away.

We didn't see Zora often; she lived a long way away, but when family came from out of town they talked about Zora— how she got bored and gave up on what she was supposed to do as the eldest daughter of Wheatland County's leading family and opened the style shop in Golden City, took off alone on buying trips east to Kansas City when it suited her. Her store was a place people could come to any time without invitation. She put out things she thought they'd like, talked and visited all day long and some days pocketed cash. She said keeping store was like giving a party.

I made my living as a lawyer for a long time, setting off every morning as Stuart used to do. I built a small practice doing environmental law, but a few years ago, I began to wonder about putting on a tie every morning. I grew sleepy in the afternoons, bored, not enough unexpected in my everyday. I wanted more company, different company, surprise. By then I knew Aunt Zora was right. I thought about that story my father had read to me about Mr. Mifflin going around in his "Parnassus on Wheels." I decided to try something like that.

So, like Aunt Zora I've become a retailer, pretty much given up my practice. I travel around visiting people and camping in the van, trading part-time in books and stories (though I hanker after some of the things Zora's sign said she sold: "Dry Goods, Fine Goods, Sundries and Haberdashery").

Between trips I'm an inspector of mornings and weather, judge of smells, full-time looker and steady reader, a writer of letters to public officials, a man of views. I love to talk, only really wake up talking. Samuel Johnson was like that. His father was a bookseller.

The stories I sell are a few of my own, mostly other people's. I keep a fold of paper in my pocket to catch what I hear as I go about, write stories down fast because they're slight and quick to fly—how people live and what they do, the risks

they take, their audacities. The universe isn't made up of
atoms, it's made up of bright fluttering stories.

This is my log and account book, the record of my first
year's bookselling work, the stories and money I've picked up
doing it.

Zora lived alone after her husband packed off. Her store
was work and family rolled into one. I've got a family.
Traveling, teaching, and selling is my work. I've worked for
money since I was twelve. Now I'm making a study of being
footloose, reading maps and books I've set aside for years.
But I need something official to set the alarm for, some purpose to be out in the world. Something I get paid to do. Liking
books and liking people who like books, I figured bookselling
was a way to get the two together.

I'm after work that will give me some high moments like
Zora's parties. I want customers coming back—"Glad to see
you made it up again"—and at some point a customer
becomes a friend in the blend of talk, sun, and breeze.

Then there's the contrast of low moments: cold, wet, hot,
sunburned, tired, scrambling to save my stuff from weather.
But awake, not half there. Nothing like a sudden rain to snap
me to attention. And there's the missionary part, talking up
reading as the magic that works us into the human continuum,
saves us from ourselves if only for a moment. I think of Sir
Philip Sidney, warm in mind for his effort to seduce a pretty
milkmaid at Saffron Walden, and her rejection: *"Good Lord,
that you should seek after so bare and country stuff abroad,
that have so costly and courtly wares at home."*

We know this story because the girl's brother saved letters
and kept the journal Virginia Woolf drew on for her "Strange
Elizabethans," an invitation to go back four hundred years
and become, in fancy at least, an Elizabethan, to discover Sir

Philip "*in his doublet and hose, his points untrus't, and his shirt lying around him.*" I like the heat in that picture.

My plan was to keep a traveling bookshop in one of those VW camper vans with a top that raises for headroom at night, hammocks built in, sink, and icebox. I'd build shelves on one side with a weather-tight cover I could lift and a bottom piece that would drop down to make a table; then I'd stock my shelves and the van's insides with four or five hundred good used books and set out. I love to eat and I love to read. I'd be a grocer or a bookseller for the same reason: when trade is off I can live on my goods.

I built that covered shelves-and-table affair and hung it on the driver's side because the other side has the sliding door. As I loaded her up, Zora began to list; I hadn't allowed for how much books weigh. I decided to try it out anyway. Zora handled like a dying guppy. In drizzle and fog, the wind drove wet in around my carefully caulked seams. The seep and damp spoiled my books. A week later I took it off.

In the borrowed van there's room for thirty boxes, maybe six hundred books. When I stop on the road I double-tier the boxes to make a sleeping space down the center. I have a sandwich-board sign, "Good Used Books Talked & Sold" in large black capitals on white; boards and sawhorses to display the boxes; warm and cold gear; a sleeping bag, pillow, and bed mat; water jug; folding chairs; and a couple of plastic sheets to drape over the tables if it rains.

I think about it all as I'm dozing off, go over my supplies like Robinson Crusoe: the food I've packed, a bottle of dark Jamaican rum (canned milk and rum poured together will warm any dreary night), routes, the sound of rain on the van roof. As I settle down, that good thing from Chaucer runs in my mind: "*Lord! this is an huge rayn! / This were a weder for to sleepen inne!*"

Jefe the dog comes along, but this peddler business is essentially light and solitary, one-on-one, unplanned, whimsical, quick, and with all that comes of quickness and lightness. It's not family work like a circus; it's more part-time. It's not independent; it's more dependent than most ways of living on what the weather is, public spaces, markets, fairs, other people's yards and tapwater, gas pumps, pay phones, public amenities, and what's at the post office.

This morning we climbed up the Berkshires to the flat, green, rocky roof of the world before we stopped. On an orange and yellow bus that passed, "There is no truth but in transit." I took that as a sign.

Franklin is a 1750s Catskills town, pretty once, but down at the heel now, the money drained away. There's a Main Street six blocks long, a fine blue stone academy at one end, a huge hall with columns (now the Masonic premises) at the other, some good redbrick stores and frame structures in between. You could shoot a Western in it.

As I drove in I sensed a bustle for the annual "Old Franklin Day," the county converging, the streets and sidewalks brisk with commerce, the weather clearing, a cheerful feeling in the air. Will they buy my books?

My friends had a table out for me in their Main Street yard. Mike and Kate have a little publishing company in Franklin, a deconsecrated bank their place of business, travelers' samples in the vault they've lost the combination to.

They were to have published one of my books once but the money ran out. Out of that disappointment we became friends. It's a strange thing. Coming to see them is a warming prospect—hugs around, mugs of coffee, news, presents. I asked about the sign I'd noticed driving in, "Peddlers Must Register," but it turns out that riffraff is exempt on the town's party day.

Kate is my age, pretty, rounded, the Edna St. Vincent Millay girl she must have been somewhat roughened now, steel-colored straight hair tied up, more dealt with than fashioned, dark colors. There is laughter in her, a willingness to be tickled. She has a sweet voice. As a high-school girl in one of these thin little towns she waited on tables weekends and then sang to the crowd for tips. Later she worked for publishers in New York, learned the trade, met Mike at one house, married him, and together they started their own company. They raised money and put together a good, solid list, but never a bestseller. You can't survive on singles and doubles in the publishing business; and then their money partner ran dry. The firm dwindles, living on its backlist and remaindering away. No new books.

Mike is seventy. The first time I met him he wore a folded marlin spike on his belt. He wears it all the time, part of getting dressed from his merchant seaman days. He went to sea at sixteen, survived torpedoings in the North Atlantic, worked as a senior editor at Macmillan and literary editor for *The Nation*. He's fair and tall, something military in his bearing, silver hair worn short, a tightly clipped mustache, perfectly turned out always, elegant.

After the war he was briefly a semi-pro boxer until he got knocked out and woke up stuttering, had to struggle to call words to his tongue. I used to wonder about his remoteness, the feeling that he'd never gone flat out with me, his guard always up, always this marvelous performance, his utterances as carefully prepared as he presented his body to the world. Now I think he kept that control to keep his tongue working.

By 10:00 A.M., I was set up in their yard and my friends were buying. "You can never have too much of *The Wealth of Nations*," said Mike, so $4 in my pocket right off. Then a homesick Englishman came by and cleaned me out of

Kipling: "Always meant to read him. Now I'm here I will."
With that another $10. Somehow *The Female Orgasm* got
slipped into one of my boxes, unsuspected and unpriced. The
man who bought *The Baseball Encyclopedia* made off with it.
"A home run," he said. Kate has an earthy laugh.

Leaving Mike in charge, Kate and I took off for lunch at
the American Legion stand and a look at the competition, the
library sale. Scrappy. No bookstores in town, not much
passed on.

Back to our stand. "Trade has not been brisk," Mike
announced. "Hardly any trade. In fact, no trade at all." Seems
he didn't get much out of his hour with Adam Smith. But by
then I'd made enough to cover gas and tolls home, so I wasn't
despairing.

We told each other and anyone in earshot about some of the
good things on our table. Mike read aloud from *Don Juan*
until the Byron was sold out from under him, then from
Tennyson until ditto. A passerby picked up our dictionary:
"$4.50 for this? It's twenty years old."

"True," said Kate, "but most of the words in it haven't been
used." Sold.

We put someone susceptible on to Oliver Wendell Holmes's
Autocrat of the Breakfast Table, one of those books you have
to be told about before you'll pick it up. Some things catch
your eye but most books you have to be put onto. Books are
like food. You grow up on a line of stuff and have to be pressed
to try something new, something strange-smelling, odd, different. You have to be told how savory it is, sold its virtues. The
best things I've ever read somebody pressed on me as if offering some surprising new part of himself: "*I was just going to
say,*" Holmes starts out, "*Audacious self-esteem, with good
ground for it, is always imposing . . . Even in common people,
conceit has the virtue of making them cheerful. . . . Talking is*

like playing on the harp, there is as much in laying the hand on the strings to stop their vibrations as in twanging them to bring out their music . . . so conversation must have its partial truths, its embellished truths, its exaggerated truths."

Then we had our apparition. Out of the afternoon light a large, powdered lady wafted by, gorgeous, fragrant, soft, rustling, layered, long strands of beads, bright paisley skirt to the ground, her hair, not yet white, pulled back and secured so firmly it pulled her face tight.

She hovered around our tables, picked up the *Rubaiyat*: "My mother read this to me. She told me to set my life's course by it."

"And did you?" asked Kate.

"Oh did I!" she said, shuddering with remembered pleasures. " *'And if the Wine you drink, the Lip you press, / End in what All begins and ends in—Yes.'* I have her copy, but yours has pictures. I'm only buying it for the pictures, so can you do better on the price?"

"Sure, 50¢ off."

That gruntled her. "You know," she said, leafing through it, "it's true what the book says, *'Heav'n but the Vision of fulfill'd Desire.'* "

She read and wandered for a bit. "And maybe I should pick up something for a friend in bed, something engaging. He bores before he blushes." To the friend's sickbed that tonic getting-up book, John Cleland's *Fanny Hill, or Memoirs of A Woman of Pleasure* in a nice edition but, sadly, no pictures.

It ended up a $60 day. Kate figured that the three of us working from 10:00 to 6:00 put in twenty-four hours. Netting our costs, we made about as much per hour as a Navajo Indian rug weaver.

Later, over beer and the dark bread and German sausage that neighborhood is famous for, Kate described George

Eliot: "The most virile mind of the nineteenth century. She had a more powerful intellect than anyone around, Dickens included. Although intellect is probably the wrong word for Dickens. He was a force of nature, like Shakespeare."

"What do you mean, 'a force of nature'?"

"There's a story about Renoir," Kate said. "A well-meaning lady at some soiree or other asked, 'M. Renoir, how do you paint?' to which he responded, 'With my prick.' That's the way Dickens wrote.

"As for Eliot, *Middlemarch* is her best book."

CHAPTER 2

My Companions

I'm in this business with my dog, Jefe, nearly every day and some days with my friend Tom. Tom is eighty-five, a schoolteacher, actor, and knife-peddler. He travels around southern Vermont selling and sharpening knives from the back of an old Land Cruiser. Tom has a lot of open time and he knows books. I pull together the stock and do all the longer runs alone because he doesn't like camping any more. "Hell! I slept out enough in the Pacific fifty years ago. Now I sleep in my trundle bed."

Every few weekends we set up together near Brattleboro. When it's quiet Tom recites poetry and tells me the stories in the books we're selling: *The Odyssey, Arabian Nights*, Shakespeare, Kipling. A little philosophy sometimes, never politics.

We tell ourselves we're in the business of putting strangers and each other onto good things—what charms it has, what fun, what truths, suspense, passion, strange sights, rarities, how gracefully written, the music in it. I made a list of what I'd stock and asked friends for their lists of favorite books, but I've learned in this business that "classic" has a lot of stretch in it. At heart it's a book that's pleased many over a long time as interesting, useful, honest, and in some way so enchanting that for a while you forget yourself.

Enchantment is the key. All the how-to books we don't stock have the first three qualities. Enchantment is what we're after, a quality like wildflowers in spring air. There's no telling where it might turn up.

I always get gifts from Tom, words no one else could give or even tell me. Somehow I can hear him, understand his urgency. My harrumphing, bearded friend, musky smelling like an old mushroom, wart-covered, not so much gray as faded, not so much bent over by age as squashed, his solidness pushed down but his excitement blooming strong. Amy Lowell herself could not have done more justice to "Patterns" than he did reciting it from memory the last time we were together. For twenty years I've carried the Oscar Williams *Pocket Book of Modern Verse* he sent me inscribed, "Dear Alan—When it's so hard to get anything decent for $2 it is a triumph of some kind to find a book like this for a quarter."

"I's satiate and clientele," Tom will say when he's happy, "Mostly okay" other times. Once I showed up at dusk, and as his house darkened he gave me from memory Lear in his madness, acted all the parts, weeping with Gloucester, "*O ruin'd piece of nature!*"

We watched the fire for a while, talked about this and that, and then, perhaps because the day was dark, Tom got onto something from Thomas Wolfe, something I'd heard him quote before: "*Naked and alone we come into exile. . . . Which of us has known his brother? Which of us has looked into his father's heart? Which of us has not remained forever prison-pent? and which of us is not forever a stranger and alone?*"

I asked if he felt alone like that.

"Sometimes at night in the quiet. By day I bustle out, push myself to be with people, wake them up, catch fire. But sometimes in the quiet, yes, I imagine my end."

Tom's hallmarks are the books he knows and quotes from and the knives he goes about New England sharpening and peddling from the back of his car like an old gypsy. He is passionate for literature—recites and professes on any occasion. Early on he invested in memory for wealth, and now he has more poetry and music than he can spend. He gives out scenes, names, and ideas in a flood. He's lived so happy for so long because he's kept working, going about doing knives, acting bit parts, seeking out and engaging people, pushing himself on the world, seeking applause and a little cash. So should we all.

Over dinner the night I showed up unexpectedly he told the story of Ali Baba and the Forty Thieves. His wife, Mary, and I sat and listened rapt like children. Later he talked about seeing a new translation of *The Odyssey*, wondered if he needed it—he has three or four—until he read the first line, "*This is the story of a man who was never at a loss.*" He bought it.

He once told me about meeting Mary. He was teaching at a new school in Putney. Late winter they gave a benefit production and Mary came. He noticed her sitting in the back, "a slight figure wrapped in a shawl like a Rumanian refugee, her bright pretty face peeping out the top. I went over to talk to her. She asked me if I'd go shares in a wheel of cheese."

What makes Tom a good teacher? Passion, impatience, memory, fury. He loves his students and hates their ignorance, rages against dullness, soars and weeps and laughs with the good things he gives, listens badly. What he has to tell us is so much better than anything we might have to tell him. I love him for his enthusiasm. Talking about Newton's genius one day, he quoted him, " '*All color comes from light and from light only.*' Wow! That just came to him." Tom's farewell whenever we part, "Good-by old thing."

Sometimes we try to sell poetry by reading aloud. It works. Tom's got a lot of good stuff committed to memory and he's actor enough to make a show of it. People stop browsing, look up surprised. "Did you like that?" he'll ask. "Here! It's a dollar." And he'll start in on something else.

I'm okay at reading aloud, not at all shy about wearing other people's wisdom, but Tom gives it drama. He'll keep reciting what he was reading after he's handed over the book.

He told me once about how he started teaching, came in one day as a substitute. The class was slogging through *Hamlet*, the kids mumbling and droopy about reading their parts aloud, unsure of what was going on. After a few minutes Tom slammed his book down and gave them the scene from memory with all the fire he had, wound up wiping spit from his mustache. "What does it mean? Act it out and you'll get what it means. It was written to be acted, just as music was written to be played, not so many beats counted out."

We push copies of the chapbooks I make up every winter on my computer—this year a collection of quotes from the *Times* and the *Spectator*, a bit from Elizabeth Bishop's "The Map," some of Vachel Lindsay's lines, a few of Walter de la Mare's, furniture from Jeremy Taylor and Sir Thomas Browne, passages from the Bible. The chapbook serves as a menu of my wares and likes and things that make me smile, like the story of Brillat-Savarin's sister Pierrette, slapped by her mother when she sang a bawdy song at her own wedding, dying at ninety-nine with the words, *"Bring me my dessert!"* Desktop publishing is bringing back the pamphlet; every bookseller can have his say again, just like in the eighteenth century.

Tom is my partner for New England; for the rest I'm on my own. Friends ask to come along, one to sell strong coffee and her homemade biscotti, another to show old movies at night—black-and-white classics from a projector rigged to the van roof and shown against an open wall. Said she might get a foundation grant to do it.

I like company for a day or two, but if someone were along full-time I'd feel responsible. My freedom to come and go, take off and hike, or mosey would be lost. I don't want to be accountable. I like to go aimless, can only do it if no one is around to notice. I'm basically lazy; a nice thing about this work is I can't get fired for it.

This for Jefe on the radio today:

> *Oh there are sober men and plenty,*
> *And drunkards barely twenty,*
> *There are men of over ninety that have never yet*
>   *kissed a girl*
>
> *But give me a ramblin' rover,*
> *Frae Orkney down to Dover,*
> *We'll roam the country over*
> *And together we'll face the world.*

—Silly Wizzard

CHAPTER 3

Learning the Trade

Tom and I tried a few afternoon bookselling sallies to get started. I lurched and rattled up to Vermont in the borrowed bus with the ground visible beneath, the horn and windshield wipers volunteering, the brakes dubious, and my load of odd lots shifting, to join in yard sales and flea markets and set up our tables on promising lawns.

One of our early sales was Virginia Woolf's first *Common Reader* right after I'd read her on Sir Thomas Browne and Montaigne. Though used at least twice I could tout her book with passion for knowing her pleasures and have come to think pimping is undervalued.

Parked outside a flea market one Sunday afternoon with the side door open to display our cartons we sold two books for $6, enough for soup but nothing for gas. It worried me that we weren't covering expenses until I thought about the whole idea of covering, and who even covers his life?

Later, Tom and I hit the Newfane Grange Used Books Tent for their closing offer: make up your own grocery bag of books for a dollar. We carried off a bag with John Aubrey's *Brief Lives*, some Boswell, and a pretty red book called *Knave Go-By: The Adventures of Jackie Nameless*, published by Oxford University Press in 1954. That book is on no list but it's so good that I'm going to republish it—the story of a young boy cast up from a shipwreck, his memory gone, only a gold locket to give a clue to his identity, and that quickly lost. It is all Dickens and Conrad and Stevenson, anxious and wonderful.

There was a big dictionary too, still fresh and working, which Tom gave me 50¢ for. Doing crosswords all the time, he burns through dictionaries like hikers run through boots.

At one of our training stops a beautiful, black-haired woman, maybe forty, maybe fifty, flounced up, blue-black ponytail flashing, short shorts, and bulging bodice. She announced herself a writer, picked up our illustrated Longfellow, advised us that she too is a Longfellow, said she used to run a show boat in England, theatricals to start, then rock and punk bands until it got too rough. Hard to tell whether our lubricious Minniehaha has a story or, like me, is making one up as she goes along. She'd got it from Tom that I was a lawyer. "I didn't think you were *really* a bookseller. Hair's too short, you're not scruffy enough. It's a class thing."

Last spring I went to London on some law business and had a Sunday to myself. I took a browse among the South Bank book tables. On the broad cobbled river margin in front of the National Theatre there were five or six waist-high trestle tables with used books rowed spines-up along the edges, face-up in the center, paperbacks mainly, good titles. A lot of people flowing slowly along, a happy hubbub of commerce.

Off to the side the two or three men who tend the tables chatted and smoked together, sipping coffees against the cool. They took the occasional money but kept apart from their browsers. One explained to me how they rent the space and set up every weekend, showed me the cupboards where the boards, trestles, and books are stored. He said he works another job during the week, buys his stock at night, does this for fun and not much profit. I asked him why he doesn't wander among his customers and talk with them:

"Lookin' at books they're talking to themselves. They don't need me."

That trip I learned a bookseller's trick. I came upon Logan Pearsall Smith's *A Treasury of English Prose* in a box at Camden Town Market, the cover swollen and stained, the price £3.50. When I quibbled the price the man whose stall it was opened the book to something good he'd marked with a tear of newspaper, warned me about judging books by their covers and took off 50p. My stock now sprouts markers like whiskers.

Recently I picked up Brewer's *Dictionary of Phrase and Fable*, the page for Caedmon marked with a tiny, delicate handkerchief: "*Famed for his Hymn preserved in Bede's Latin. Bede says he was an ignorant man knowing nothing of poetry, but was commanded in a dream, by an angel, to sing the Creation, which he straightway did.*"

I bought a *Bartlett's Familiar Quotations* for $3, a fifteen hundred page university commenced in 1855 by a Boston bookseller to bulk up his trade—my copy on India paper, fresh still after fifty years. Christopher Morley opens the eleventh edition: "*What is the quality of permanence that makes it worth while to pack in our scanty baggage, for one more trudging hike forward, the remarks of our predecessors?*" The evening I bought the *Bartlett* I lost myself in "these personal outcries, wrung from men and women in the strong twist of life," finally coming to at midnight to Jefe's loudly rattled importunings for a few moments outside.

How can I sell these books? I already have a *Bartlett*, but leafing through this one I ticked things I never noticed in my own, and every book is like that: I read around in the ones I've priced and stacked for sale and discover things. If I read or reread every book I mean to carry I won't get off this summer or next, or ever. Maybe that's the stuff of fantasy: you play it out in your imagining but never leave unless, like Stevenson, you're driven by health or crisis.

My collection is the sum of my personality—better than I am surely but true to what I admire and aim for at my best. I like it when someone comes by and discovers for himself one of my treasures. I like reading aloud the high notes and stunning starts of things like that early passage in David Copperfield, *"I was born with a caul...."* That makes my hair stand up.

Tom and I steal things from our boxes. Every now and then Tom will find something and head off to his truck muttering, "I'll just take this on approval." Such was the case with the *Oxford Book of Ballads* last Sunday. But that's his pay, he gets no other.

Sometimes a friend will ask to borrow something I've put out. I quit lending when I overheard a borrower remark of one of my strays, "Why should I rush to give it back? He's only going to sell it."

Henceforth books appeared to him no longer as merchandise, as dead commercial objects, but as beings endowed with reason, whose strange fate and careers merit the attention and sympathy of every thinking person in a much higher degree than a thousand other things to which in our time so great an importance is attached. Now he understood the old saying: Habent sua fata libelli—*Books have their fates!*

—Julius R. Haarhaus, *The Assembly of Books*

CHAPTER 4

Memorial Day Weekend

Off to Brattleboro in the groaning van, thirty-five cartons of books aboard, plastic dropcloths in case it rains, four sawhorses with four long pine boards and an old door to make up tables, my backpack, Jefe in his box, Milk Bones, and a jug of water. The van is brim full, the tires splayed and noisy. Jefe and I bus along high up this bright spring morning, gear-shifting, happy in the fragrance of wild white roses and honeysuckle billowing on the roadsides. A seven-hour poke to "Bratt" with time out for Jefe's salutes and addresses, my own, and now and then revivals. We both think ice cream is a swell revival. A shared cone creates a bond.

There's no radio in Zora so as I drive along I sing to myself and run songs in my head. When we camp I sometimes play notes on my harmonica, long lines of sound I like to hear. Thoreau used to take his flute out on Walden Pond and play to the fish, drew them to his boat.

I miss the radio. As a boy I used to watch it. We had a big Magnavox with a green eye that opened as you tuned in. During the Depression people would give up everything before they'd give up their radios. My father worked for an engineer who realized that somebody could make a good living fixing them, so he made up kits to teach people radio repair by mail. As his boss explained the kits, my father wrote the lessons and then the ads. Box #1 got you started with a soldering iron, a plain chassis, some radio parts, wire, and a lesson on how to make a good connection. With the second box you made your own circuit tester. Then more complicated things until Box #10 arrived with all the parts to build the Super Receiver. At the end you got a certificate and you could set up in business. My brothers and I took the courses over the years—built radios, sensors, electric door locks, alarms, motors. Sometimes the stuff we built caught fire.

The lady who owns Solar Hill on Western Avenue said we could set up in her yard. As we pulled up, I saw she'd mowed the lower part for us, left it fuzzy like a meadow. There's a tree we can sit under. We're at the foot of a long, steep hill rising to a fringe of tall pines and, on top, a pink-shingled house with round porches and white columns that used to be Mark Hopkins College. A dirt road runs down lumpy and dusty to a pile of rocks and a mailbox where the dirt road meets the paved. That's where I'll set up my sign. I noticed something gold in the grass by the mailbox, a little gold foil square. A nicely packaged Japanese condom. This must be the place.

When Tom showed up he looked at the loaded van and asked, "What's the rated load of that thing?"

"Rated load?"

"Tare and tret."

"Tare and tret?"

"How much does it weight empty—tare—and what's the maximum weight it's supposed to carry—tret?"

I'd picked a place to camp, a fairly grassy spot beside North Pond. The breeze ripples the water and sets it lapping. The pond is surrounded by a fringe of hills, at dusk the body of a Lachaise woman, large and dark and curled around the water admiring her reflection. The sun sets on legs rising to thighs, to rump, slope to waist, chest upswelling, fine roundnesses of breasts. A nice fragrance of wintergreen underfoot.

There are signs around, "Public Water Supply, No Camping, No Swimming." Lawyer that I am I struggled with that, answering the charge by saying that since I was living out of the van, I wasn't really camping. The sign made me uneasy for a while but other things like dinner took command of mind.

I gathered wood, made a hot little fire with a small earthquake candle for a starter since the stuff I found was damp. That fire-starting earthquake candle was cheating. My brothers taught me how to make a fire by holding a magnifying glass to catch the sun just right, beaming it on leaves and twigs and bits of birch bark to make them smoke and smolder and eventually flame. If the sun was low we'd use a mirror. They taught me how to signal with the mirror too, how to survive alone. I like the idea of it, but I talk with more self-reliant independence than I feel. The hours I dreamed over Walden and Outermost House I left out imagining how lonely I'd be after a few days. When I sell those books, I'll warn what lies they tell.

I settled my coffee pot and another for goulash. Jefe laid claim to the extra goulash with a leaping, yipping aggressive caper unbecoming a merchant's dog. The fire smelled good, the cooking smells were good, Jefe went exploring, I leaned back, well pleased. But not to read. Camping like this doesn't lend itself to reading. There's a lot of busyness in setting up, I'm usually dirty and tired, and then it gets dark.

A strange thing it is to sit quietly outdoors in candlelight. The five flames I set out are nervous and jumpy, but sometimes their flames are tall, shapely, finely colored, and tapering. The cheap ones go down fast, dripping and guttering in the slight breeze, so out and goodnight to a smoky smell that reminds me of church. I crawled into the van.

I couldn't drop off. I heard things, remembered things I had to do, scrawled notes to myself, felt achy on the hard bed. It was stuffy in the van, musty, dusty, dog- and book-smelling.

Jefe settled into a hot lump beside me. My space was so narrow I couldn't really shift, turn over, adjust myself; it was all-or-nothing, back, side, or belly, no in-between. I got up and set my tent on the pond shore. Amazing how exquisitely sensitive we are to slope and slant, and funny how direct the feel of the earth is when you lie down on her. The slope of feet-to-shore felt strange, and for all my foam mat's merits, roots and rocks intruded. There is no smooth in camping out. The princess was right about that pea.

I awakened, tangled in nylon, to a voice and Jefe's frantic barking. I didn't know where I was. At last I made out a man in uniform. He said something about camping, permits, high fire area. Dawn was beginning. I said I'd go.

The air smells good. I set up the Gaz, soon had a good coffee going and food out for Jefe. The dawn is warming the hills I watched last night. As the light comes up they stir and shift, an altogether different figure from last night's.

I warmed a little pan of water for shaving, but suddenly it seemed silly to do so little with the pond beckoning. I was outside the law already, so, sign or no, I stripped and made a run for it, hit the cold, found myself out before I'd splashed my knees.

Fresh clothes for my first big sale day, orange pants, dark pink shirt. They'll be able to see me okay.

> *And then he stretched out in the sun,*
> *And rolled upon his back for fun!*
> *He kicked his legs and roared for joy*
> *Because the sun was shining down!*
> *He said he was a little boy*
> *And wouldn't work for any clown!*
> *He ran and laughed behind a bee;*
> *And danced for very ecstasy.*

—James Stephens, "In the Poppy Field"

CHAPTER 5

In Business

As we arranged our tables under the maple, Tom talked about how we're starting a school here just like the first one—a teacher under a tree with a book and someone curious. Then Mary banged up in her old Ranger with jars of flowers for our tables, a jug of cold tea, a hamper of sandwiches, and a box of bright India-cotton bedspreads to swag the tables. She said we ought to wear costumes and funny hats to get people to stop.

Once I put out my sign people started coming over. Quarters and dollars began to fill my pocket. At one point, Tom stood back and looked over our array, the flowers, the fluttering cloths, the two or three browsers: "Do you know *The Rubaiyat of Omar Khayyam*? Remember where he talks about wine and then remarks, *'I wonder often what the vintners buy one half so precious as the stuff they sell'*?" Like the old vintners, Tom and I laid aside a couple of good things for ourselves to brighten the night.

Over a picnic of savories and laughter, Mary produced a bag of hats "appropriate for booksellers" to mug in. We talked about joining a flea market, but the one at Newfane costs $20 and setting up alone in a pretty spot on a traveled road seems more promising. We decided our browsers don't go to flea markets. They seem more readers than scavengers, although I'm both, and so is Tom. Our trade happens by, tucks in when they see the sign and the flutter of our four trestle tables bright

24

with India-print bedspreads. I put a $4 ad in the *Town Crier*
but the only person who mentioned it was a dealer who
bought nothing.

A lull—bells, insects churring, white flowers in the field—I
lay down in the van. Tom read "Dover Beach" aloud. Then I
heard him quote to someone from *The Practical Cogitator:*
*"What to keep in the face of calamity? Not a bar of gold, a com-
forting book like this one."* It went. I got up when Jefe sounded
an alarm: a very stout lady wheeled in on a bicycle, cheerful
and glowing. She told us she works at The Retreat downtown,
a place for mental patients: "First time I've ever really felt good
about working." After a lot of picking and choosing, she took
the *Medieval Reader* for a Christmas present, said she'd buy
more, "but after back surgery and at my weight—I know I look
ludicrous on this thing—I can't manage another package." Said
she'd come back. I hope she does; she's a sweetie.

The sun beat down curling some of our book covers, then it
showered a little, spotting the others—all to make our good
used books look a little more goodly used. The dog dozed in
his box; Tom snoozed in the driver's seat. We took in $40.

As Tom browsed over our boxes of stories he pulled out
one and handed it to me: "A most wonderful book, *The
Woman of Andros*, Thornton Wilder, and look what a well-
made thing it is, laid paper still fresh, Albert & Charles Boni,
New York, 1930. I loved it." I set it aside to find out why and
became hooked by what I happened upon: *"She cited often the
saying of Plato that the true philosophers are the young men
of their age. 'Not,' she would add, 'because they do it very
well; but because they rush upon ideas with their whole soul.
Later one philosophizes for praise, or for apology, or because
it is a complicated intellectual game.'"*

It takes about an hour to pack up. We usually start around
5:00 P.M., hauling the heavy sandwich-board sign in at the end

to top off the load. The sign, which remains out while we lug boxes into the sagging van, always seems to excite a few last passers-by who fear they may never have this chance again. Today a man drove up close, left the engine running as he scurried over to ask if we have golf, gun, or fishing books. I'd just bought an old Modern Library *Compleat Angler*, went right to it, handed it to him anticipating his delight. "No, no, something bigger. Pictures!"

Did we break even? We couldn't replace what we sold for what we got, but we couldn't buy some of it either: the talk, found books, found friends, clouds, meadow flowers, crickets. We made enough to cover gas and tolls and a fine dinner with reviving mugs of sweet porter and a thick chop bone for Jefe that set him growling with pleasure all night. There are books enough left to sell tomorrow. We're long on Mary Renault, Laurie Lee, Thoreau, Boswell and Johnson, and our stuff looks old. We've got to get some newer titles and scare up some mysteries since they were much asked for.

Maybe bookselling is a comedown. We were meant to be authors, teachers at least, but this feels lucky, even if it isn't a real business. It's a calling. Our stoppers-by get the benefit of our browsing and wandering; we get an excuse for both, plus the pleasure of talking with new friends. It's like dealing in treasure. The other day I found the Norton two-volume *World Literature Anthology*, three thousand pages of fine paper for $7.50, now offered at half a cent per page.

One browser picked up *Moby Dick*, gingerly, half-afraid. "Oh, a most wonderful book! All America is in there," Tom exclaimed, "Queequeg, Pip, Starbuck, Tashtego, Ahab. Their ship, the *Pequod*, is America herself, searching for her destiny. And so many stories! They kill a whale and tie it to the ship for the cutting-up and trying the oil; Tashtego falls into the cavernous body; how Queequeg jumps overboard with a knife in his teeth to save him. . . ." By this point, our looker was clutching the book like it might take wing, or explode, or both. But she bought it. A certain garrulousness is a virtue in this business.

Plays languish. Not much commerce in plays. I was about to dump the lot, but Tom said to read George Bernard Shaw's prefaces, especially his preface to *Androcles and the Lion.* I pulled that one out. I like it when someone pushes something on me. It's curious, the potency of a negative comment about a book or author, much stronger than praise. Most of us welcome an excuse not to deal with still another voice.

Sunday was a $100 day, a dollar of that from my pressing Warner's *Beautiful Swimmers* on a man who came by looking for botany and wandered off with blue crabs, the "Jimmy and the sook," watermen, and the Chesapeake Bay. I got another dollar from selling a book of Kipling stories to a woman who asked for summer reading. We are outfitters to the mind.

Kipling sells well here. He lived in Brattleboro for a few years around the turn of the century, imagined *The Jungle Books* out of this Vermont green. *Kim* is my favorite: a boy like Huck Finn off alone on a great river guided by an older innocent. We collected $4 on our Kiplings, buying us two mugs of Moonbeam Ale at Latches Grille downtown.

We were loading up on Sunday, deep into the sweaty, gritty heave-and-haul part of our day when a motorcycle roared up, dusting our road and frightening the dog. A man got off, slight, done up in black, helmet, glasses. I couldn't see his eyes or make out much of his face. He stalked around our tables (must be the boots and road cramps that give them that Hells Angels gait), found a book, a Bible. "Have you any more like this?" he asked in a voice unbecoming his outfit. "No." The helmet came off, the glasses, the sinister. He was maybe twenty. "I'll take it. I'm glad you've got the King

James, the Authorized. After that The Enemy got it." I agreed, told him I used to go to the Episcopal church, but no more. They've switched to the new Bible. I grew up on the old music; the new doesn't have the same magic for me. He smiled and nodded, passed out some little scripture quotes on salvation, and took off.

Monday was quiet and threatening rain. People don't buy at the end of a holiday weekend—they haven't got much try-something-new optimism then. We had time to sit under our tree and read, took in $12 before the rain started in earnest, decided that if that's a typical day it's almost okay. When there's a lull or bad weather, Tom is good company.

From memory all of a sudden the other afternoon, he offered the start of *The Canterbury Tales*, along with what "sniggling" means: "That's what's so wonderful about English! A word for eel catching." I asked him for his favorite word. "Today only, 'frangible.'"

Bluets, wild strawberries, and buttercups in our field, and late, even in the rain, crickets already.

> *Tom, this fumbling through other minds*
> *Has made me thirsty. Tell me where one finds*
> *A place where you and I can sit,*
> *And slake the dust of other people's wit.*
> *Alan, I know a tavern not too distant*
> *Where we can sit and talk o'er wine consistent*
> *With our own thoughts; and while we're drinking*
> *We will atone for all vicarious thinking.*

> —After Charles P. Curtis, Jr.,
> and Ferris Greenslet
> *The Practical Cogitator*, 1945

CHAPTER 6

The Stock

The books I'm carrying are ones I've read and want to read again and things friends have told me about with so much urgency or awe I watch for them like people I want to meet. But some of the best I'd never heard of before I came upon them—small press and out-of-prints that look promising, books on no list, things never mentioned in passing. I hadn't bargained for what I'd find in books I didn't know.

Example: *The Pauline Muses*, a comely, brief anthology nicely made and brightly bound in 1947, prose and verse written by fifty-two former members of St. Paul's School, among them Edmund Halley of comet fame. Halley is represented by his letter to Sir Isaac Newton trying to persuade him to publish the *Principia* (which Halley saw through the press at his own expense). I look for books like that, anthologies and commonplaces.

On my want list is another copy of John Aubrey's *Brief Lives*. Aubrey, like Boswell after him, hungered to hear, had a gift for listening and remembering. Aubrey is vivid to me for being so credulous and susceptible, so forthcoming about his unsureness, so desperate for memory. There is a longing wistfulness in his *Lives*, as if by telling them he could keep his friends and warm himself remembering.

Some of that heat carries still. Of Sir Walter Raleigh: *"Queen Elizabeth loved to have all the servants of her Court proper men, and . . . Sir W.R.'s gracefull presence was no meane recommendation to him . . . His voice was small . . . He loved a wench well; and one time getting up one of the Mayds of Honour against a tree in a Wood ('twas his first lady), who seemed at first boarding to be something fearfull of her Honour, and modest, she cryed, Sweet Sir Walter, what doe you me ask? Will you undoe me? Nay, sweet Sir Walter! Sweet . Sir Walter! Sir Walter! At last, as the danger and the pleasure at the same time grew higher, she cryed in the extacy, Swisser Swatter! Swisser Swatter! She proved with child, and I doubt not but this hero tooke care of them both, as also that the Product was more than an ordinary mortal."*

I went to George Allen's used bookshop one day as I was starting to collect my stock. "Do you have *Middlemarch?*"

"*Middlemarch* the novel? No. We have eight or nine books about *Middlemarch*, several biographies of George Eliot, half a dozen books about *Middlemarch* and the feminist Zeitgeist, but the book itself? No. We don't carry fiction. You'll have to go somewhere else. Now Trollope, we've got a lot of Trollope, we can do Trollope for you."

He said I could take from his toss-outs anything I wanted for my truck, but I was sure to starve on it and get dirty in the process. I said I'd find surprising things to read. He looked up: "If *that's* what you're after, try the library."

Going over George's toss-out boxes is like opening presents. The ratio of keepers to rejects is about the same: 1:10. As I do it, I ask myself, will we ever do away with books? For all the technology since Gutenberg, were he to come back today he'd recognize the book and know exactly how to use it. I can't imagine life without books—dozing off dreaming to a comfortable little computer.

I once heard a wonderful lecture, "Works of Art, Too, Have Careers and Adventures," about the peregrinations of a few of

Josephine Napoleon's beads, some of Drake's trading truck, an ancient carved crystal vase. For my part, I'd tell about a book I came upon in one of George's boxes, a finely made book about London, published there in 1951, and bearing on the inside cover a small bookseller's label from a shop in Johannesburg. On the flyleaf, three prices from as many shops. There was a gift inscription dated 1954, another from 1957, and several owners' names. Hardly a secondhand. It must be a fourth or fifth, with stories of its own: forty years of being shipped, sold, given away, mailed, and lugged, with tales of booksellers, shelves, borrowings, browsings, and how many readers that had handled and possessed it. It can claim as many lovers as an old courtesan. This time around it ended up in the sun-creased hands of a large, pleasant woman on her way home to Montana.

Most of what I carry is priced under $10. I mark up twice what I pay. Good stock is hard to find cheap. The fair copies are bought by collectors who shelve them for the mystery of appreciation, the worn ones ignored, often tossed out. I spend ten hours traveling around collecting for every hour selling. I've pulled thirty feet of books from my own shelves, easy enough as I have to weed my library to move anyway, but still a pang—will I find the like again? (as I put a selection of Byron's letters into one of my sale boxes).

The challenge is to get strangers to take on my rummages. Students of any age are the most willing: "Look, if you like that, this book will take your heart"—pressing Carr's *A Month in the Country* on a man who'd picked up Laurie Lee's *As I Walked Out One Midsummer Morning*; a paperback of Montaigne's *Essays* to an immense, red-faced Central Vermont Railroad freight man named Gordon who said he was eager for good books to fill his layover hours. His wife had just started community college. He said he was afraid if he didn't start reading "the big stuff" they wouldn't have much to talk about. "You got two or three different kinds of books," he said as he left, "Classics like Shakespeare, Blake, and Coleridge; the Greeks and Romans; and Everything Else is books I've never heard of but you must like."

Someone was looking for *God's Snake* (not on our tables), said he supported himself as a civil engineer but is starting over, going back to school at forty to become a schoolteacher to boys like himself who grew up angry and did drugs. ("The Vietnam War, too much testosterone—kids today have their own reasons every bit as good as mine.") He's studying African-American literature because that's where the jobs are, picked out a bag of books he'd like to teach. "I can sit still and read now—like to get others into it." He learned to read as his father read *Kim* aloud. When he scattered the old man's ashes, he read aloud the parts his father had liked best.

For ballast I've got Kipling, Dickens, Shakespeare, Boswell's *Life of Johnson, Don Quixote, Huckleberry Finn, Kim, Travels with a Donkey, A Tour of the Hebrides.* For a while I carried those travel books in good, well-made editions, laid out some real money for them. No takers. The Penguin versions, on the other hand, skip right along.

Penguins are my staples. Even the old ones in pale blue covers with browning paper sell—titles like *Medieval People*, with thirty inspired pages on Marco Polo. A lot of Modern Library titles are in my rolling university too, along with Viking Portables and any of the series of Oxford Books Of . . . that I can find (The Sea, Death, Friendship, the Victorians, etc.)—I can't keep them. My boxes (cut down to house the books spines-up) are marked Stories, Biography, Travel, History, Natural History, Autobiography, Journals and Letters, and Catchall. M.F.K. Fisher and the Bible fall into "Catchall," along with poetry.

In "Catchall" one day there was a 1921 Boni & Liveright edition of Walt Whitman's *Poems*, tan leatherette with a rambling, friendly introduction by Carl Sandburg: "*It is the most intensely personal book in American literature, living grandly to its promissory line, 'who touches this touches a man,' spilling its multitude of confessions with the bravery of a first-rate autobiography. . . . 'Leaves of Grass' is a book to be owned, kept, loaned, fought over, and read till it is dog-eared and dirty all over.*" I like the story that when they autopsied Whitman, the doctors were astounded that he'd held out so long given his diseased liver, pleurisyed lungs, swollen heart, and ruined joints: the man was used up.

One of my customers put me on to Logan Pearsall Smith's *Unforgotten Years*, wonderful for the story of Whitman coming over from Camden to visit the Smiths in Germantown for a month at a time: "*He had the habit of singing 'Old Jim Crow' when not occupied in conversation, and his loud and cheerful voice could be heard echoing every morning from the bathroom or the water closet. His arrivals were always unannounced; he would appear when he liked, stay as long as he liked; and then one morning we would find at breakfast a penciled note to say that he had departed early, having had for the present enough of our society.*"

Another "Catchall" book was the Fowler brothers' *Oxford Dictionary*, bound in dark blue and a good size for holding, the paper still white after forty years and much use for its advertising at the start its "*unprecedented abundance of illustrative quotation: define, and your reader gets a silhouette; illustrate, and he has it 'in the round' . . . common words that no one goes through the day without using scores or hundreds of times, often disposed of in a line or two on the ground that they are plain and simple and that every one knows all about them by the light of nature, but in fact entangled with other words in so*

*many alliances and antipathies during their perpetual knocking
about the world that the idiomatic use of them is far from easy."*
Its back was broken. I paid a dollar, glued it up, sold it for four.
I've got three or four times more stories than anything else,
maybe the true proportion of imagination to life, like salt to
seawater. When he set out on his Andes trek, Patrick Leigh
Fermor carried *Nicholas Nickleby* and *Kim* and rejoiced when
he discovered a companion who might trade an *Oliver Twist*.
Why are we so drawn to stories? I think Christopher Morley
got it right: *"Lord! When you sell a man a book you don't sell
him just twelve ounces of paper and ink and glue—you sell
him a whole new life. Love and friendship and humor and
ships at sea by night—there's all heaven and earth in a book,
a real book I mean."*

For my part, letters, journals, and autobiography make the
best reading. However he may present himself, a person
telling his own story is compelled, desperate to make a record
or set it straight, shape what happened. Grass grows over in a
season and memories dim, but the writing gets clearer and
clearer. Ultimately, all writing is autobiography, and when
writing his life a man can't be careful. Risks are everything,
the letting-in. There is more of Dickens's life in *David
Copperfield* than in all the books written about him. I lug a lot
of Dickens. And a sleeper I like to press on the susceptible,
John Buchan's *Pilgrim's Way* for his outdoor boyhood in
Scotland and fine pages on hiking.

I go for good solid stuff fit for a mind to be seen in, fit to
take in, and take inside. Ask a man what he reads and you'll
know his soul. After a certain age, we read to find and confirm
ourselves; we read our friends. What I have over my competition is that I've read or I'm willing to read the books I carry,
things so good they ought to be read. Once I learned to read I
was never alone again.

One day I had only a few books out as rain loomed, no visitors for a long while, then a boy on a bike came by. I showed him *Memoirs of Hadrian*. He took it and then asked me, "Of what you have left, what one book do I have to have?" *Irish Fairy Stories* was popped into his bike pouch when I pointed him to this: Finn McCool asks his warrior band what is the best sound in the world: "*'The cuckoo calling from a tree,' says Ossian; 'The ring of a spear on a shield,' says stout-hearted Oscar; 'The laugh of a gleeful girl,' says another. 'They are good sounds all,' said Finn. 'Tell us, chief,' one ventured, 'what do you think?' 'The music of what happens,' said the great Finn, 'that is the finest music in the world.'*"

I felt a few splatters, then the heavens opened. The boy helped me spread the plastics. I hadn't figured on what the wind would do. It lifted those sheets like skirts. As we scrambled for rocks to hold them down I noticed the water was ponding, pushing the centers down, pulling the edges up. We did what we could, then retreated with the shivering dog into the bus. A nice clatter on the metal roof but it sure didn't sound cheerful right then.

I toweled off Jefe and told him it would let up in twenty minutes. It did, more or less, and my friend pedaled away. I scrambled my drooping boxes into the van. The wet books began swelling. Boxes that had held twenty dry barely held ten wet. I couldn't fit everything in, had to stash my sign, sawhorses, planks, and boards in the nearby woods. Then the van wouldn't start. I ran it out to the road on the starter, got a little roll going backwards, kicked it going. What with the soaked books, the wet cardboard, the dampened dog, my own sweat, we were fragrant in there.

Back at Tom's I saved out the dry books, put a fan on those that showed only a little damp, and threw away about a third of what I'd had out. Even the ones that were only slightly wet

ended up so puffed and buckled their covers wouldn't lie flat.
The Oregon Trail looked like it had made that trip.

1st Gent.   *How class your man?—as better than the most*
                Or, seeming better, worse beneath that cloak?
                As saint or knave, pilgrim or hypocrite?

2d Gent.   *Nay, tell me how you class your wealth of books,*
                The drifted relics of all time. As well
                Sort them at once by size and livery:
                Vellum, tall copies, and the common calf
                Will hardly cover more diversity
                Than all your labels cunningly devised
                To class your unread authors.

                        —George Eliot, *Middlemarch*

CHAPTER 7

The Bargain

I know I can't live on it, but if I'm lucky my sales will cover replacement stock, gas, and repairs. Eke is a wonderful word. In the safety of my pension I imagine a life of eking along, nothing extra, stripped down like Appalachian Trail through-hikers, except that they know their living so is an exception. To truly eke is to have no certainty of anything more. I am eking now. It's scary and exhilarating, even though my income is above the poverty standard for a family of four. Some standard!

I don't pay more taxes than the government takes on its own, and I don't buy insurance beyond what I need to drive the truck. As my body breaks down in small ways I buy repairs out of pocket; something big and I'll take my freedom. I wish I had one of those national health cards Clinton tried to get for us.

For now I'm fitting together four or five things I like to do: travel around lightly, gather stories people tell when they're talking easily, shop for books, teach a little while talking books. The trick is to live rich any way you can, to buy little, eat low, take trips, give and find pleasure, and make books even if they aren't half buckram. I'm lawyer enough to know I'm a remainderman and life tenant only; my use is what matters.

In his *Journal* Henry Thoreau asks, *"What is the color of the world?"* and in the next breath he worries about making a living. I worry about that, too—how to make a living living.

Thoreau surveyed, taught school, and shoveled manure to pay
his way and eventually concluded that so far as his economy
was concerned, *"My greatest skill has been to want but little."*
Somewhere else he wrote, *"A man is rich in proportion to the
things he can do without."*

In *The Compleat Angler*, Izaak Walton tells how *"Diogenes
walked on a day, with his friend, to see a country fair; where he
saw ribbons, and looking glasses, and nut-crackers, and fiddles,
and hobby-horses, and many other gimcracks; and, having
observed them and all the other finnimbruns that make a complete country fair, he said to his friend, 'Lord, how many things
there are in the world of which Diogenes hath no need!'"*

About the time I was growing restless in my office I got a
questionnaire from my law school asking how I was enjoying
my profession, what I'd done, what service, how much I was
making. The problem is that I don't think of myself as a
lawyer any more than I think of Izaak Walton as an iron-
monger. In my mind's eye I've always been a journalist. The
law is how I get my keep. It never became for me the calling
it was for my grandfather or the old men I clerked for in
Providence.

What had I expected? the form wanted to know. Well, nothing. My virtue and my defect is that I've never been totally
committed to any one thing. What I hadn't expected was how
important work would become to me, the very *doing*, the
sense of purpose and justification in it. Work as a product, not
a cost or a burden.

Selling *A Garlic Testament* one afternoon, I got to talking
about work with one of my customers. He told me how he
once asked his Dickinson College students to write their parents' biographies and how surprised he was at how eager the
parents were to join in. One student wrote about his mother
who came from Russia and supported the family when they

arrived by trimming hats in Shamoken. He explained how important hats were to the immigrants: in Russia the peasant women wore babushkas; in America they could dress like ladies—they were ladies—and ladies wore hats. Her work was to help them become Americans!

Over beer and dinner one night Tom and I talked about saving: what a mistake it is. We agreed that it's a far better thing to spend yourself down all along—body, goods, and purse—and die spent. The best law teacher I ever had gave as his life's rule: "What I gave away I kept; what I spent I had; what I saved I lost."

In the ideal exchange I'm after a little cash and something of your story. Everybody has a story. Some are surprising, like the old man who showed me the dinosaur tracks near his home. I've discovered there's no quicker way to make friends than to ask someone for his story, best of all to ask, "How did you learn to read?"

I like showing people what a varied and beautiful thing a book can be. Never mind how battered, used, and traveled: pay attention to its shape and smell and heft, its size and style of type, how its page appears—margins, gutters, leading, the color and weight and feel of its paper, the fragrance of print in a new book, the scents and signs of its past in an old one—tobacco and cognac, or onions, basements, and foxing depending on its fortunes. Consider the way the whole is held together: signatures, stitching, binding, the fineness of buckram, the care in paper covers. When I was twelve my father's bookseller initiated me into these mysteries. She'd hand me a new book, open it carefully, push it close to my face saying, "Here, *smell* this!"

The shapes of books are as various as the shapes of people. I like best a narrow rectangle, light, white paper, the whole not heavy, perhaps an inch thick, pictures sometimes but not in stories. Let the words paint people, scenery, and dogs. It matters how a book opens, how the pages lie. Does it give itself with a fight, a struggle, or a graceful and delighted yielding? I used to be a publisher. I think book making is as fine an art as book writing. I've caught the bookseller's disease. My discrimination is weakening. I've come to believe that there are few bad books. Most books have something because most authors are passionate in their work. They did it for love, most of them, knowing well enough that they'd never be paid in the coin that buys bread. They wrote out of compulsion, driven by ego or religious fervor or a sense of beauty, to illuminate life. Henry Miller said of his books, "They were alive and they spoke to me." One loves or loathes an author depending on his soul— how similar or striking it is in comparison to one's own. For pleasure one reads one's friends.

If I spent as much time reading as I do looking for books I might get somewhere. But I'm not looking for the book I know, I'm after the sleeper I've never heard of, a classic that will tell me where I want to get to, a *Book of Answers* (I'd settle for *Leading Questions*), or a story or journal so compelling that it makes questions and answers irrelevant for a while. A collector knows what he wants. I don't.

When I was a boy I thought I might end up as a printer or a minister, but Stuart warned me I'd starve at the first, and by the time I got to junior high school I realized I wasn't suited for the church. This work combines something of both so I'm taking it. It's time: The men in my family don't make seventy. I read with rinsed eyes the other day something one of Elizabeth's seamen wrote her in a petition: "*The wings of man's life are plumed with the feathers of death.*" Emerson said that true economy consists not in saving the coal, but in using the heat while it burns.

Consider the economics of this business (I like the idea of a science of money, fools' poetry): I carry about five hundred books marked $2 to $12.50, with an average profit of $3. If I sell them all that's a $1500 gain over replacement cost—a couple of months' gas and food and the value of the books we sneak to our own shelves. Can I count on selling five or ten books a day? Will I find what I need to restock? Nice worries, a manageable struggle, not abstract like my legal things. I can see my personal wolf from the door, admire his teeth, gloat each day I cheat him.

I hope my sign and boxes attract friends. People of all ages come up to me and start talking when I'm out walking the dog, and Jefe is along to help. I keep a calendar of who to put in with now and then for what that ancient vagrant, my imagined forebear John Aubrey called his "sweet otiums," his leisures. For me these are a hot shower, washed clothes, and a home-cooked meal. In exchange I try to brighten my friends' time with stories, good quotes, and good titles.

Without too much worry about permits, sales tax, or vendor licenses, I put out my sign and open up where yard owners let me and see what trade I draw I'm welcome like an old-time peddler with his rare goods, Vachel Lindsay faring with his bag of poems.

Winter is for whatever part-time schoolteaching work I can pick up, book buying, and holing up. Eventually my routine will be to head down South as spring breaks to make Mississippi in ploughing time, then follow the warmth north to town squares and farmers' markets, finally joining up with Tom around New Haven.

Who uses the word peddler anymore? Or tramp or hobo? "Itinerant" conjures up the homeless, but formerly it had to do with journeying—a person who alternated between wandering and working. That's my plan, to live like the Friars, "act-

ing the part of itinerant preachers." In the old days they called
merchants like me "travelers" and spoke of what I do as
"shifting" goods. That all feels about right.

I'm happy in the summertime
Beneath the bright blue sky
No thinkin' in the mornin'
Where at night I'll have to lie
In barn or bire or anywhere
Dozin' oot amang the hay
And if the weather please me fair,
I'm happy every day.

—"Tramps & Hawkers," Scots song

CHAPTER 8

Heading Home

Heading home on a whistle I'm amazed I've lived so long. A couple of times I've given myself up. I used to be more rooted, more fixed, but time and the wash of events gradually dissolved my foundations. I'm traveling lighter and lighter. Things lay claim. Sorting books for the van is a good discipline, a lesson in utility: Is this worth lugging? I go out with less every time.

The house I'm moving from is eight miles from Philadelphia. I have the endings of an old garden and the beginnings of a new one there, weeds beyond number. There's a lot I'll miss. My college, Haverford, is across the street. Sometimes at night I hear laughter, students' voices, bits of music. Other nights I'm aware of frogs on a pond nearby, ducks gossiping, the low fluttering whistle of owls, sounds that were there before farms, railroad, or college. It's pretty much a tame place with lights, crickets, and glowing squares from ship-like houses moored up and down the road. As I pack up to move away, I'm seeing it all with new eyes. I bustle about to keep from thinking too much right now. "Bustle" makes me smile for Samuel Johnson's definition: "going about a ship on horseback."

Jefe and I bump along high up in the van with gears to work, a cool breeze behind with fine spring airs, fragrances of sweet pea, honey locust, and catalpa, whiffs of diesel. I've never had more fun driving anything. Near Bridgeport a faint but palpable sea mist, not yet fog, rolled in bearing sea scents, then linden and thistle and loose-strife, and at dusk the rich evening offering of skunks. Zora is loose and rattly; I'm always startled to see the road rushing below.

I'm carrying a load of Vermont wall stones and a carton of books I just bought on a bargain. Among them is *The Oxford Book of the Sea* with something from Robert Cushman Murphy's *Logbook for Grace*—the letters he wrote at twenty to his bride of a few days about sailing off on an old whaler to study Antarctic birds. She gave him a bag of letters on his departure, one for every day of the year he'd be away. His recount the pleasures of reading hers and the log of his days. There's a note at the end about the whaler's fate: pressed into cargo service during World War I to carry dry beans to Europe, the brig sprang a leak in a North Atlantic storm. Her beans swelled, the Daisy burst.

Passing through Northampton I looked at a repainted VW camper on a lot—a '75, no rust, $4,300, the speedometer stopped at 99999.9—I think it's been there before. The ship-cabin interior is rounded, all its space put to use with cabinets and squirrel holes, the hammock rolled and stored overhead, sink, toilet, holding tank, water storage, ice chest, but all worn down, loose, frayed, and stale-smelling. Is it bargain enough to take on and struggle to keep going? There is oil under the motor. This one is probably a Californian, many times around the world before she picked up her orange coat and beached here. I could live in her okay, but where would I put the books?

People ask if I mind all the driving that goes with this. I mind the cost (about twenty-five cents a mile) and how it makes my legs cramp sometimes. I can't do more than two hours without a stretch. But driving along I sing, whistle, and think about the people who came by. Yesterday there was something about a Zen master visiting a Pacific coast retreat.

The master worked on the lawn with his archery teacher, practicing shot after shot, steady tension, concentration on the target, perfect aim. Then he turned toward the ocean and let fly. "Bull's eye!"

Sometimes I think about opening a shop. Setting up and tearing down every day is hard work. It would be nice to have a place that people could come to when they wanted. I picture the bookshop my father used to take me to, a cozy made-over brick house in Georgetown called The Francis Scott Key. It was run by a big, friendly woman named Marty Johnson. She gave me "totin' rights" when I was ten—said I could carry home, free, any return or ex-rental that caught my eye. She would press on me books she liked—E.B. White, Edith Hamilton, John Steinbeck. "You suck mud, and you'll never get rich," Marty said of her business. But she carried it on with scotch and cigarettes and a few small legacies—five thousand titles in three downstairs rooms. She lived over the store. Four women worked there, two of them volunteers happy for the company of customers, books, each other, and smokes and booze together.

But I'm not ready to keep a shop. A couple of years ago I found a "For Rent" sign on part of Haverford Station. I called the next morning, my heart pounding. They wanted $15,000 a year on a tight lease. That broke me of the idea. I thought of all the books I'd have to sell to pay the rent, how many hours I'd have to sit indoors. It's the prospect of sitting tight in one place that I don't like. I'd miss the traveling around too much. Everything I do is in little pieces.

I mark our progress crossing creeks and rivers in this land galleon, square-rigged and roaring like a storm, tossing the wind aside and leaving in our wake dust, swirled leaves, and gusts, progressing south river by river—the Connecticut,

Farmington, Quinnipiac, Housatonic, Sheldrake, Byram, Hudson, Passiac, Hackensack, Raritan, Delaware, Schuylkill. Jefe figures our progress in his own way. As we go into the steep turns off the Merritt Parkway, he wakes and announces his intentions about a visit to the posts and yards at the Visitors Center. Then he's set for New Jersey. South on I-95 now. We can keep up with the big trucks okay. Power's not a problem with Zora, control is. She wanders on her own in a dead calm; truck wakes send her dancing like Jefe around a big dog. So we pick our times for traveling on 95 and where we'll stop. Off to Route 1 and the Princeton Diner this afternoon, something I've promised myself for the last hour. They bake their own coconut cream pies, the best I've ever tasted.

Yesterday I got some books free from a friend who'd heard about Zora and wanted to clear his shelves: five Kiplings, *The Strange Lives of Familiar Insects*, and something called *Animal Navigation*. I like natural history. *"They sell best of all books here,"* Peter Collinson wrote to his friend Linneaus in the mid eighteenth century from London. That's not quite true for me. I stock a lot more than I sell, push them as part of my missionary work, especially Sally Carrighar titles. Her *One Day at Teton Marsh* is the best of its kind: one day in the life of a water strider, otter, hawk, and some others at a mountain stream in late fall, the turning time to winter. Unsentimental, vivid, beautiful, violent: the stuff of life.

When I was in high school I learned printing and got a job clerking in a Brentano's Bookstore. The manager confided in me that he'd only lately come into the book business. He'd been a D.C. Transit bus driver, but one hot afternoon the traffic, buzzers, and tourist questions got to him. He stopped his bus mid-route, ordered the passengers out, drove to Baltimore, and spent his change draw on a good meal. He had the admirable belief that to sell books his clerks should read them, encouraged us to take home, compliments of the house, titles we found interesting. So my library began.

I was learning to set type in shop class at school, set some poems I liked—Yeats's "Song of Wandering Aengus" and "Lake Isle of Innisfree"—in large Bodoni and printed copies on big sheets of colored paper. My Brentano's manager let me sell what I'd printed and keep the proceeds.

Cranbury, New Jersey, is a pretty name and the town has a good secondhand bookstore, a lucky place for me as it turned out. I came upon *A Treasury of the World's Great Letters* (1940), the print still fresh on good laid paper. At the start were a dozen testimonials "In Praise of Letters," the first from Voltaire: *"The post is the consolation of life."* Five hundred and sixty-three pages: Alexander the Great to King Darius (*"The King of Heaven has bestowed on me the dominion of the earth . . ."*), John Keats to Fanny Brawne (*"But if you will fully love me, though there may be some fire, 'twill not be more than we can bear when moistened and bedewed with Pleasures . . ."*), and this from the editor's commentary on Diogenes to Aristippus: *"The only record of a meeting between Alexander and Diogenes is the historic episode which took place in Athens, when the Emperor, encountering Diogenes by chance, asked how he could serve him. 'You can stand out of my light,' Diogenes answered. The reply so impressed the conqueror with the contentment of Diogenes that he walked away exclaiming to himself that if he were not Alexander he would like to be Diogenes."* I gave the price of a *New York Times* for it.

I struggle over what to buy for Zora, what to carry, how to choose. The best teaching is how to choose what's best. Making up my book boxes is a little like my father working up his radio repair kits: boxes to teach the culture.

Montaigne set out in 1571 to read and speculate in a library of one thousand volumes, an extraordinary collection in his time, worth a fortune. One hundred and fifty years later Samuel Johnson's bookseller father gave his son the only fortune he had, one hundred books, when his boy departed for Oxford. By comparison my vanload of books cost very little. One of the wonders of the Industrial Age is cheap books. Honor William Caxton, the first publisher in England, the Henry Ford of books. He died the year Columbus aimed west off the Canaries.

I'm lucky to be starting this business in the age of canons. A lot of talk and writing now about what people ought to read, lists, what's important. I have my take. I'm tempted to put on clerical garb, at least the collar, and hang clergy plates on Zora. When I told a friend what I had in mind, he said, "Try a hearse, you'll make more of a splash. Put Sydney Smith's motto on the side in gold, *Tenui musam meditamur avena* (We cultivate literature on a little oatmeal). No parking problems, no hassles in traffic!" I told him I thought it would attract the wrong trade.

> *Good morning America,*
> *how are you?*
> *Don't you know me?*
> *I'm your native son.*
> *I'm the train they call*
> *the city of New Orleans,*
> *I'll be gone 500 miles*
> *when the day is done.*
>
> —Steve Goodman

CHAPTER 9

Fourth of July Weekend

I've finished my move to Hatfield, Massachusetts, to a small, old white Yankee box with a slate roof. The lot is 65 feet wide, 2 acres deep. There's a tobacco barn out back. We've fixed it up and made a room with bookshelves for me and a big studio for Martha downstairs. We overlook a swamp that's good for birds and then the long, narrow field and woodlot that for a hundred years supported the families that lived here. From one of my plant books come the names of the potatoes I'll set next spring: Maris Piper, Belle de Frontenay, Binges, King Edward, Kennebunk, Red Norlands.

The lanky guy next door with a dead cigar stub in his mouth and pants that look to be falling off keeps sulky horses in his field, nervous, delicate creatures, nodding and tossing at one another when they're close together, almost dancing. He doesn't ride them, no one can. They're his pets. He comes out from work at noon to feed and water them. They know the sound of his jeep, run around when they hear him coming.

Only an hour's drive up to Brattleboro this morning. Hazy and warm at 6:00 A.M. It smells of milkweed and wild roses. It's going to be hot, in the 90s.

Tom was waiting for me on our hill with a thermos of strong coffee and a couple of Mary's pizzas, still warm. Very fine at 7:00 A.M. He had a new word for me, accidie.

The lady who owns the hill must have had it mowed yes-terday. This morning it is ridged and humped like a piece of rough green cardboard.

I hauled and dragged our heavy sign down to the road. That goes out first because it rides on top of the load. We want the early Farmers' Market callers driving by to start thinking about us.

I lug and Tom arranges. He's not really a good grocer, doesn't rush to display our meats and vegetables. He snuffs and marvels over them, then lurches guiltily into activity only to stall and dawdle again, reading. Amy Kelly's *Eleanor of Aquitaine* caught him in her embrace this morning. He read aloud her rare account of what led up to Becket's murder and then the thing itself: "*Thomas, the man of God, in the dim hour of vespers and on the very steps of the altar of Canterbury, had shed the red blood of the martyrs. . . . Thomas, finding the world too small a place for both himself and the king, had stood up to death for his salvo.*"

Fifteen volumes of the Harvard Classics in Zora this morn-ing. I got them for $15. The one volume of *Prefaces and Prologues to Famous Books ("No part of a book is so intimate as the Preface")* is worth that price. Here are Caxton, Calvin, Copernicus, Newton's Preface to his *Principia*, Samuel Johnson's to his *Dictionary*, Whitman's to his *Leaves*, and more. The sixty-second edition is printed on good rag paper and well-bound. If I had to settle today for one set of books to carry into exile the Harvard Classics would be it.

As I arranged our wares I picked out titles for a friend in Philadelphia. I don't have a standing order from him but I have a feel for what he likes and how fast he reads. When he retired from his law practice he took up history. I tried him on Gibbon. He read it all in a gulp and hinted he'd take more, so every six weeks we meet for lunch and I present him with a grocery bag of five or six books I think he'll like, plus a sleeper. We pretend that our lunches are social. He doesn't look into his bag until later. Then I get his check and a note about what he's kept. What he doesn't want he returns the next time we meet. His checks average thirty dollars. Delivering those bags is fun. Bill acts as if I'm making him a present and insists on paying for lunch. So far this morning I've picked out *Memoirs of Hadrian* and Wright Morris's *Mississippi Reader*. The sleeper this time is Jacquetta Hawks's *A Land*, a book about England with an odd, out-of-place early chapter, "An Aside on Consciousness," musing on evolution and the occurrence of moments of genius like Proust, Newton, Einstein, and Mozart.

I had a good sweat going and three of our four tables pretty well filled when a fine tall girl arrived on a bike. She was in a school tee-shirt and had a long auburn braid. She looked cool and crisp, unheated from her ride. She gave Jefe her early attentions, which pleased him so much he accompanied her on her rounds.

She told me about a couple of the books she'd read in college this year, picked up another copy of one for a gift, Carlo Levi's *Christ Stopped at Eboli*. I happened upon Kilvert's *Diary*, opened it to what I'd marked, the entry for 13 July 1871. I walked over and read it to her: *"As I sat at breakfast I heard the drone of bagpipes. A man was playing at the New Inn. He came playing down the road and stopped in front of the forge droning on while the blacksmith's children danced before him. He could not complain that he had piped to the Clyro children and they had not danced. He was a wild swarthy Italian-looking man, young, with a steeple-crowned hat, and full of uncouth cries and strange outland words. He moved on from the forge to the inn still playing while the children still danced before him. I could see the group through the screen of chestnuts."*

A tall, gaunt, white-haired man heaved up. Tom knew him and did the first accosting. The newcomer had already picked up one of our staples, Whitman's *Specimen Days*. Right away he and Tom were off on the great self-taught authors: Shakespeare, Cervantes, Dickens, Melville, Whitman, Kipling, Yeats, Dostoyevski. Tom's friend's name is English. He's a poet. "They learned in the streets," he said of the self-taughts, "in the army, on the long roads. They read people. The originals do that. The others read books and make embroideries."

Tom huffed some exceptions but English held to his embroidery.

"It can be rare stuff," he allowed of Tom's exceptions. "You've got Eliot, Pound, and Merwin here. Wilbur. They're good. But they're feeders on books. They never manage the shock an original wrests from life. They never get that close. Close enough to get scorched."

English left with *Specimen Days* and what he said were two of the more original books on our tables, Charles Olson's *Call Me Ishmael* and William Carlos Williams's *In the American Grain*.

The girl paid for her Levi and Kilvert. "I can see why you two do this," she said as she stuffed her books into the bike bag. "'Good Used Books Talked and Sold'—the operative word is Talked."

It's 10:45, $35 already; $65 if I count what I'll get from Bill.

Tom showed me something in a Christopher Morley book he'd picked up, a long essay about reading called *Ex Libris Carissimis*. At the end Morley lists his favorite books, offering his list as a gift like the one Petrarch left in his will, "*To his dear friend Boccaccio, fifty golden florins for a winter gown for his evening studies. 'Surely little enough for so great*

a man.' " Tom took off for a lie-down, said he'd be back with
Mary and lunch around 1:00.

There were four or five people studying our tables. No
one looked like he needed help or even looked approach-
able. I'm not shy about pushing myself on people or asking
for things. What do I have to lose? But today I don't have the
oomph to do it. The heat's worn me down, and I'm hungry.
I peeled an orange, downed the last of the morning's coffee,
gave Jefe a drink.

One of my callers came up to pay. He was a wiry black-
haired man in his forties, hair thick on his arms and tufting out
around his collar. He had Hemingway's *Death in the
Afternoon*, a copy with a small Braque print tipped in. He said
maybe he'd found a rare edition. I don't know. I'd marked it
$10, couldn't remember where I'd gotten it. I showed him
another Hemingway.

"This one's a bigger bargain," I said, handing him *A
Moveable Feast*. "He talks about writing. He's young, he's in
Paris, he's broke, it's cold, he goes off every morning to an
unheated room. There are wood stick matches and the smell
of burning orange peels in it, cafés, and a writer's trick he
came on: leaving off before he'd finished a passage to have a
thread to pick up the next morning. Overall there's the smell
and heat of the woman he returns to after his stint."

That sold it. I'll miss it.

An older woman was hobbling around. Big, a long face
with straying silver hair, well-dressed, a necklace of pale
gold links. She'd picked up the three volumes of Sigrid
Undset's *Kristin Lavransdatter*, handed them to me to hold
while she went over another table. She had a cane but she
was impatient with it, pegged around quickly with a slanting
lurch. One leg is longer than the other. "Is this a fund
raiser?" she asked. "You can't be making much money.

You're out of state. Do the people who own this place know you're here?"

She's over seventy, bright eyes, an accent, abrupt in a twinkling, friendly way, doesn't seem to expect answers as she drifts off before I can reply to her questions.

"You must have a problem with people walking off with books."

She said her name is Lise, offered $5 for my $10 Undset. "I'm Norwegian, I've read it. I'm buying it for my granddaughter. She ought to read it but I bet she won't. It's old fashioned. I'm the only person you'll see today who's read it. I'm certainly the only person who'll offer to buy it. You! Have you read it?"

"No."

Tom and Mary were pulling up. I said okay to her offer if she'd tell us over lunch how she happened to turn up in Brattleboro in our borrowed yard on a summer afternoon in July.

She laughed, pleased with the idea of selling her story.

"Is this an interview?"

"Yes," I said, getting out my pen and the damp fold of paper from my pocket. "I'm going to take notes."

"What do you do with what people tell you?"

"I'm a journalist. I keep a journal."

"Why a journal about strangers?"

"We're all strangers, more or less."

She joined our picnic. In bits and pieces over a couple of hours, as we got up to tend to customers and people flowed in and out of the conversation, she told us about the aunt who'd sent her to America just before the war. The aunt was an opera singer in Austria who'd taken the girl on a spring skiing party in the Alps. "We skied bare-breasted, rouged our nipples," she laughed. "There was a count in the party. He wanted to marry me," she said half-dreaming. But we never heard how she ended up in Brattleboro. During a spurt of business she left with a wave.

A tall, older man in thick glasses and new running shoes arrived. It was late afternoon. There were some early July 4th booms. "Sounds authentic," he remarked. He was smoking a small cigar. There'd been a story in the paper that morning about the Enola Gay and the atomic bombs we'd dropped fifty years ago. Tom was talking with someone about it. There was some loud back-and-forth about our using it.

The tall man took in the talking as he browsed a table. I asked him what he thought. He straightened up.

"Pro." He spoke slowly, firmly. He'd thought about this, talked it out before. "I was a Marine on Okinawa. We were marshaling for the invasion of the home islands. We had some new troops. It was mail call. As I heard the bomb news I happened to look over at a fresh-faced boy who'd just arrived, his new rifle in one hand and a box of Baby Ruths in the other. It went through my mind that he just might make it back to whomever had sent him the candy."

The day's total came to $169. By 7:00, when I finally pulled up the sign, I was wet with sweat and itchy. Headed off to Sunset Lake for another prohibited dunk. Two fishermen were far out in a canoe. There was a family around an illegal campfire up from where I parked. I stripped in the van. Left Jefe inside. Slowly slipped into the water. Didn't splash or swim, just gasped and soaked for a few minutes in the shocking cold. Warmer than Memorial Day. I heard a car coming. Zipped out and headed home.

Sunday morning we set out five long tables but we never got them all loaded. We had two of them swagged with gaudy

African cottons and pretty well charged when a broad-chested man drove up—forties, small eyes, an antique dealer who specializes in paper.

He looked around for a little while. I wandered over to say good morning.

"What's your situation?" he asked.

I told him. "What's yours?"

"Used to be a stockbroker, gave it up seven years ago. It got to where I didn't like pushing people to buy securities they didn't need or shouldn't own." Now he goes out and finds the paper they ask him for.

I showed him a small, finely made two-volume set of Virgil's *Georgics*, a little battered but a handsome thing still.

"Nope, not for me. I avoid the classics. They don't sell."

He's a professional, picks his books like he picked his stocks. Knows exactly what he's after. I'm an amateur. Everything's in my line. Or nearly. I do shy away from books about politics and religion.

He carried a want list and found something on it, an odd volume of Churchill's *History of the English Speaking People*. He was pleased with his bargain so I thought I'd stretch him a little, showed him V.S. Pritchett's *A Cab at the Door*, a memoir of growing up in England as the son of a grandly high-minded and impecunious linen and ladies' underwear merchant who practiced Christian Science and left the rent unpaid. Pritchett's clearest early memory was of a cab at the door for the family's next move. My man was dubious but he took it.

Tom turned up a small volume of John Suckling's poems, one of a broken set. Suckling had a hard life and his book was worn, its hinges shaky.

He held it up: "Look how loved this book has been, how used!"

"Suckling was a pretty man," he continued, showing us the engraving at the front. "It was a time of pretty men. Raleigh, Lovelace, they wore their hair like girls and they were regarded as men when they were still fair and beardless."

He read some lines about a woman whose finger was so slender a gold ring burdened it, her feet so delicate they slipped out from under her skirts betimes like mice.

A young man reached for it.

"Nope, not for sale," Tom said. "I have to keep this one."

He sat, worrying a loose tooth, in his chair under the maple. His teeth are pretty ragged and this one is the lower front-most, always aslant, now looming forward with its moorings rotted. It got to his temper.

Someone passed close by murmuring to her companion, "I don't have time to read any more. I have too many books anyway."

"Then why the hell are you here?" Tom harrumphed. "Why did you stop? Go on! Go on!"

They recognized him from town. "Well, Tom, we do like looking."

A trim, gray-bearded gentleman walked over smiling. "I sell used books too. Just off Washington Square. I get kids telling me that now, students, 'Too many books, no time to read.' Or they complain they can't afford something I have. I tell 'em, 'Go to the library, get it free.' Often as not they'll say, 'But I want to own it.'"

Tom laughed. "That's the secret we can't let out! It's all free at the library."

We introduced around. The New York bookseller's name is Page. He told us he'd been a social worker for twenty years. Gave it up when he felt he wasn't reaching his clients.

"Class, age, language, it all came apart. We had less and less in common. The kids I was dealing with weren't kids like

I had known. My adult clients didn't trust me either, they were foreign. So I gave it up, took my pension, spent my savings on fixtures and stock. Now I'm into this kind of social work."

We'd been at it for a couple of hours, had a nice steady trade going, when Jefe came over to me looking worried. He'd heard it first. A far-off rumble. It was just beginning to cloud over. He hates thunderstorms. I put him in his box in the van and got out my plastics. I figured we had at least another half-hour before the rain.

Tom and Page were having a good legs-out talk about New York in the old days. Business was brisking along, my pockets filling, trade spiced a little by the coming storm.

A sturdy, brown-haired man came by asking for children's stories, books for kids age six to sixteen. I showed him our Kiplings and Stevensons and he took them all, but he asked for a bargain. He had large eyes and a wonderful smile, easy and open with fine, large white teeth. His name is MacIntosh. He explained that he's a private school teacher in Springfield, Massachusetts, working for his master's degree. He's spending the summer on a state program working as a counselor at a camp for Pequot Indian youngsters. He wants stuff his kids can read on their own and he can read aloud. He doesn't have a budget. The state money he gets is barely enough to live on and keep his car insured. He's buying books for his campers out of his own pocket.

Tom was delighted, his tooth forgotten. "I'll cover you!" he yelled as he bustled around grabbing titles. "What a good thing to be doing with your summer!" He picked up a couple of anthologies, a book of short stories, a *Robinson Crusoe*.

The thunder was getting closer. Page and MacIntosh helped us spread the plastics and weight them down with stones which Mary had heaped up around the mailbox for such an emergency. The rest of our little crowd disappeared. The four of us moved under the maple.

Tom told us about going over to the Brattleboro Retreat every Tuesday night to read and tell stories to the young people there, kids in trouble. They're sent by the Juvenile Court. He gave us from memory some of the things he's given them: the start of Alfred Noyes's "The Highwaymen" and Walter de la Mare's "The Listeners." Mac scribbled titles in his notebook. In one of the anthologies Page found W.E. Henley's "Invictus" and gave him this for his charges: "*It matters not how strait the gate, / How charged with punishments the scroll, / I am the master of my fate: / I am the captain of my soul.*"

"Concentrate on reading aloud," Page advised. "Good to have books around they can read on their own, but after lunch or a hike break, when they're a little tired, relaxed, that's the time to read aloud. *Robinson Crusoe*—start with that. A young man cast off, scared, alone, inventing everything himself as he makes his way. Kids understand that. That's how they see themselves."

"And *Captains Courageous*," said Tom, "a chapter a day. Wonderful stuff!"

"What about Native American stories?" Mac asked.

Rain was noisy in the leaves overhead. I remembered Frank Waters's *The Man Who Killed the Deer* out under one of the plastics. I told Mac some of the story: New Mexico in the early 1900s, the feel and smell of the pueblo, the desert and the mountains in it, a sacred blue lake, the young Indian in trouble with the white man's law for killing a deer. Mac's eyes widened. I scooted out for it. Somehow I went right to the book I wanted.

The rain spit and splattered and looked black for another twenty minutes, but the lightning never got very close and then the storm veered off.

Mary arrived with a picnic hamper. There's always more than enough in Mary's baskets, so Mac and Page stayed put. Jefe waxed very friendly over the remains of a pork chop. We peeled back the plastics. Things dried off and our crowd picked up again. Mac headed back to camp with a bag to which we'd added *Notes of a Biology Watcher* along with *One Day at Teton Marsh*. Page covered those last two. Tom put down his money, Page his, and Mac his share. It came to $33 after I took off $6.

At my suggestion Mary settled down with Sacheverell Sitwell's *The Gothick North*. When I pointed her to his paragraphs about *"The delayed climax of the armoured man . . . the final and most extreme point reached by Gothick fantasy,"* Polish horsemen clad in wings five feet long made of gray eagle plumes fastened to the shoulder and down the back, she was lost in a minute.

Mac and Page took off. Business stilled. It was overcast and muggy now. Hard to tell whether the booms I was hearing were July 4th foreplay or thunder. Jefe was wide-eyed, wouldn't leave his box. We figured the storm was circling back.

We loaded the books, hauled up the sign, and counted the day's takings—$154 in small bills and change. All the dollar bills we get here look like wilted lettuce. We never get crisp new money. People must feel easier spending the spent stuff.

Mary wanted to go to the Packers Corners' Fourth of July fete, a potluck with music and a home-grown production of *Under Milkwood*. Tom said he was pooped. He offered to take Jefe home with him, so I went off with Mary.

The Packers Corners commune has been around for twenty-five years. Mary had befriended the pioneers when they came out from Boston University in the '60s despairing of politics, a group of musicians and lit and theater majors who pooled what they had and took on a run-down farm. Mary helped them raise vegetables and sell the surplus of what they grew and made, gave them a recipe for apple pie. When apples were long they'd stay up all night before Farmers' Market days baking in an old "Home Comfort" wood stove. Their stand had a sign, "Life Is Short, Eat More Pie."

The storm had finished and the air was new by the time Mary and I arrived. There were fragrances of the sacred herb and knots of talkers. A lot of talk about Vietnam around us. Overheard: "I was more into politics than sex then."

A stage had been rigged in front of the barn. There were songs, stories, jokes, and skits, but the best came at the end when the children were whirling sparklers out in the orchard. All you could see were circles of white. A curly-haired pioneer who played guitar announced, "This last one's for Mary Panzera." He sang with a friend in close harmony, "Wild Mountain Thyme."

Mary smiled, waved, then closed her eyes and rocked and sang along softly:

> *Will you come lassie come?*
> *And we'll all go together*
> *To pick wild mountain thyme*
> *All around the blooming heather.*
> *Will you come, lassie, come?*

CHAPTER 10

To Westerly

I'm up by 5:00 A.M. most mornings, hauling out from under a mountain of covers, stumbling around until the coffee takes hold, then to the door for the weather, "So! Good morning, God!" Darker now at 5:00 than it was a month ago, the air damp and fragrant. Spider weavings on the grass and hedges.

I loaded the van last night, a half-load this time, twenty cartons, maybe four hundred books. I usually stuff in all I can, more than I have room to display, wind up putting boxes on the ground and leaving some in the van. But I'm off to Westerly, Rhode Island, for a crafts fair this morning— "Things made by hand, and books"—have only a small rented table to display my stuff. At heart I'm an inventory junkie (most used-book dealers are). I like to show everything I have, despair when a customer might like something I know I have but don't have handy. It's not the lost sale I lament so much, it's the missed chance to put together a book and its rightful owner.

I resolve all the time to control my collecting, to limit my stock to what I can display at any one time. But then there's the Ludington Library sale near my old home in Haverford or a chance to buy a good lot from an estate or a yard sale I happen upon. A few days ago, a friend called and said, "I have some things for you, can you come by tonight?" Of course. I'm addicted to food and books, tuck in to every good meal I can because I don't know when I'll get another. A chance at good books is the same kind of thing. When hunger was an everyday possibility (in Pepys's time, in Samuel Johnson's) the prospect of a good feed had its right value. Ditto when books were rare. For me a good meal is a kind of wealth and a heap of good books is Social Security.

I packed a borrowed tape deck to music my way to the coast, oranges and roasted almonds (the best travel foods), and Alpo and dog vitamins. Took Jefe out for a brief walk around for the necessaries and by 6:00 we were off. Two months ago I sent the fair organizers $50 for my space. I used to visit a summer home just up the coast. I like the idea of spending a night there again.

An hour and a half down to New Haven. Yale is quiet in mid-August, almost still. I parked in front of the law school. The gates were open, so I let Jefe jog and mark the courtyard. Coffee, a look at the paper, then the van wouldn't start. Sometimes after a hot drive it shuts down for a few hours. Nothing to do but wait it out with a walk.

I'd leashed Jefe and was locking up when a cleanly dressed man crossed the street toward us. "Can you give me a quarter for breakfast?"

I nodded and handed him the quarter.

He looked at me. "You could do more."

"I did what you asked."

He walked away. As Jefe and I walked around I thought about my duty to him.

After New Haven, the road to Westerly reaches east and north through rocky green land rouged in patches with red grass. Pretty names to me, Old Saybrook, Lyme, Chester. When I started this business I thought I'd open up in one of these Connecticut towns. But it turns out they're too polished, too rich to have need of me. Good used-book towns have some scrappy yards, an institution or college that attracts reading workers, young people, scruffy elders. Few people with big incomes are big readers. The sleek cars that pull up leave with little.

We skirted around Westerly to Route 1, an American song-line beading the coast towns together, Boston to Providence to Westerly to New York, Philadelphia, Baltimore, Charleston, Savannah. This was the post road Benjamin Franklin traveled when he was postmaster. Some of the houses he might have seen still stand.

I buy odd volumes of *The Franklin Papers* whenever I can. Last night as I packed one of these I looked for references to Westerly. There's a 1772 letter Franklin wrote from London to Joshua Babcock, a local doctor: "*I thought often of the happiness of New England, where every man is a freeholder, has a vote in public affairs, lives in a tidy, warm house, has plenty of good food and fuel, with whole clothes from head to foot, the manufactures perhaps of his own family. Long may they continue in this situation!*" On May 4, 1776, Dr. Babcock voted to repeal the Act of Allegiance to King George. He was sixty-nine years old, prosperous, and prominent. There was risk in his treason.

Noon: I parked by the entrance to the private beach I used to visit. A notice warns that they tow unregistered cars found inside. I leashed Jefe and we walked the mile to the water. I figured I'd swim and scout the area for camping later.

The beach comes up suddenly on a faint line of salt mist. There's a path off the road through wild roses, then you drop down to the water over big granites. The waves are surprisingly loud. They frighten the dog. He's not altogether welcome here. Neither am I, clothed and unfamiliar, but he is on leash and I look middle-class. And, anyway, the fringe reached by tide water is state land. We get glanced at but nobody nods or engages eyes. We headed over to a rocky

spot, well away from the sunbathers. I try to interest Jefe in
the water. No thanks. I stripped down and headed in. Jefe
barked but wouldn't follow. It's a nice shock, seventy-degree
water against the ninety-degree air. Blood and the sea's salt
levels are the same so it's right that the ocean smells of life.
Life is surprisingly salty. Any animal eating me won't have to
add any. I wasn't in long. Somebody walked over to see what
the dog was yelling about. Jefe grinned as I clambered out:
"Saved you, idiot!"
     There's a salt pond on the other side of the parking lot. No
one around. A good place to dry off and read. As Jefe and I sat
sunning on a big rock, a swan coasted out on the pond. I
sneezed and she leapt from the water shaking out three-foot
wings like sheets flapping. From Henry Miller's *Big Sur* (the
book in my hand), *"All I can say is: Clarify your position!"*
     Jefe began to droop a few minutes underway on our walk
back to the van. He's more a sprinter than long-distance trot-
ter, and he's bored with this track. He worked out all the good
scats on the way in. I wound a sling out of my jacket and carried him like an African baby on my hip. He half-dozed in the
rhythm of walking, roused only by a passing car. A few cars
passed, but no one offered a ride. The only folks who walk
this road are the few who park outside to use the beach during
the day. We are not to be encouraged. I'm too proud to hitch
now. I hitched a lot when I was a boy in Silver Spring. The
most successful hitchhiker I ever met was Mull, an English
boy I camped with once. Mull would face the zooming cars in
South Africa with his pack at his feet and lean way out into the
road juggling three bright balls.
     I'd left the van near a restaurant with a beer garden. It was
early and the heavy, toiling, old lady waitress said it would be
okay if Jefe sat out there with me. On her own she brought
him a platter of meat scraps. Altogether satisfactory, as Tom

would say. I was itchy after my swim. With an unnecessary
"Stay!" to my companion, who wouldn't have left that plate
for an earthquake, I ducked into the bathroom to sponge off
some salt.

We drove back to the beach again at dusk. The parking lot
gate was new. I hadn't noticed it before, pushed back into the
bushes. We were locked out. I drove back to the restaurant and
parked again. I didn't want to worry all night about getting
towed. For a moment I thought about a motel, but motels are
pricey in season, and anyway I wanted to sleep by the water.

I filled my pack and remade the belly-sling to carry Jefe.
The trip down to the beach was like going back down the
mountain: every step painful, the exhilaration and variety of
the climb replaced by a stumbling numbness. No cars passed.
A long slog through the green- and sea-smelling summer
night air down to the beach where every cottage has its mailbox out by the road tagged with a family name, and then a
strange thing—an open garage with a light on at the far end
where a man was sitting on a stool, his back to me, bent over
a plank on two sawhorses.

The water was quiet. I leveled a bed in the sand up by the
rocks and set the tent, a tiny bright blue one-person affair. The
returning tide, whenever it comes, won't reach up here.

It's cool enough in the sea breeze, and there are enough
bugs around that to sleep inside the tent will be pleasant. A lot
of stars. I can make out some of the figures but I don't know
their stories. I always wanted a light at night until my cousin
Faith pointed out that even the darkest night is never black.

I crawled in and zipped the net shut. No need to close the
flap; I like being able to look out at the sky. Lay down on my
sleeping bag and wiggled around to make the sand fit my
frame. But the mold once made stays fixed, so you have to go
through the wriggle routine every time you shift around. I

shifted a lot. A slight breeze off the water rattled and ruffled the nylon. The steady sea noises were soothing. I got comfortable, felt safe and sleepy. Floating like a large warm chip at my feet Jefe waited out all my adjustings. Then he burrowed down beside me, made a few noises of pleasure and sighed deeply. He has a sea-dog smell tonight.

The old ones, mostly men, come down at dawn to fish and walk the beach. A few come with their dogs. It was an early dog, snuffling and then peeing on our tent that got Jefe going. All hope of sleep ended as he tore at the netting to defend us. It was almost 6:00 A.M.

I was cold and coffeeless, struggling to empty my tent of the sharp breeze that was making a wind sock of it when a lanky old man appeared in bright fluttering jogging satins and a sun hat tied under his chin. Jefe was busy running down gulls, yip-yipping in the high, authoritative voice that poodles have a patent on. I was advised that camping on the beach and dogs off leash are not allowed. He was nice about it, helped me mash the air out of the tent. His name is Cort. I told him what I was doing and asked him to come see me at the fair.

He ended up inviting us over to his cottage for breakfast. Pushing him a little, I asked about the possibility of a shower and shave. That granted, maybe he'd watch Jefe while I took a quick swim. Okay. I ran into the water. It was a lot colder than yesterday, North Pond cold. "Bracing" is the word for swimming that knocks your breath out and knots your parts.

Cort has a dog too. After he and Jefe did their cordials Cort supplied a want I'd forgotten last night: dogfood. Breakfast for me was coffee and a Rhode Island specialty, "johnny-cakes," cornmeal patties about the size of silver dollars fried thin and brown and served with sausage and maple syrup.

Cort is an investor, works his portfolio by phone and computer for a few hours every morning, spends the rest of the day on the beach. He was a partner in a big New York house. He has a son my age, a songwriter and folksinger. I asked about his son's songs, how the politics in them fit with his own. "I do what I do because I like making money. Sidney does what he does because he likes making music. We get along okay, but we don't share the same American Dream. Why do you sell books? A hobby? It can't be a real business on the scale you seem to be working."

I allowed as how I'm touchy about "hobby" getting tied to what I'm doing. Cort laughed and said he's touchy about the politics in Sidney's songs. So we did our cordials. Then he asked, "You're lonely? No family?"

"No, I've got family," I explained. "But I'm hungry. I've got good company in my family and in my books. But I like town life. Contact with people and new experiences wake me up, put me onto things. Zora introduces me to people I might have something in common with, folks who'll sharpen my politics, sing me poetry, tell me mysteries and stories, put me onto books I don't know. And maybe I can do the same for them. A friend just wrote me, 'A man's work should have the seriousness of a work of nature.' In terms of eating every day what I'm doing isn't that kind of work, but opening people to pleasure, that's important. That meets the test."

"Sounds to me like teaching is your calling," Cort said. "Do you know Borrow's *Bible in Spain*? He went out in the mid nineteenth century to peddle and give away bibles. Didn't have an easy time of it. Not a lot of demand. In some places the priests would kick him out. He might give you some ideas. And what do you know about Johnny Appleseed? Another of the "Joyful Noise" persuasion.

Carried Swedenborg tracts in his pack, tore off pages for folks he stayed with and sold apples to. He showed up once at a tent revival in Ohio, heard someone yelling for the barefoot sinner on his way to heaven. Johnny stuck out his leg and yelled, 'Here I be!' "

This sounded a little far afield for an investment banker. Turned out Cort has an interest in Catholic missionary work, visits missions. But before we got very far into that a nurse came in. His wife lives in a wing of their cottage cared for day and night, an Alzheimer's victim. "She looks younger and more beautiful than she did twenty years ago," he told me, "but she doesn't recognize me any more, or Sidney. She says her brother's name over and over again for hours, calling for him sometimes like she's lost."

Cort drove us back to the van. We passed the garage where I'd seen the man sitting on a stool last night. I asked about him.

"That's Mac McCloud. He was practicing piano. He's a music professor in Missouri, comes here every summer. He's afraid the neighbors wouldn't like to hear his practicing so he plays a board marked with the keys. Says he can hear it all in his head. Whenever there's a sea storm he goes down to the beach and leans into it. Last hurricane they had to pull him off."

As Cort let us out: "I'll come by later. Let me see what you have on the American Dream."

I started setting up around 8:30. I was late. Most of the other crafts and book people were already established and trading with one another. I was assigned a table next to the fountain, surprised to get such a good place until the first strong breeze sent a mist over.

The book dealers are grouped together. There are about twenty of us on a large open pavement around the fountain. The paths leading off from our circle are lined with other vendors. Some old-fashioned slat benches have been pulled around into the spaces between the dealers. The place has a good feel to it. Tom had been telling me our shop needed a name, it wasn't enough to announce "Good Used Books Talked & Sold," we had to say whose. So I crayoned "ZORA'S" in red on top of the sandwich board. No sooner did I have it up but a lovely young French woman wanted to know "Who—or what—is Zora? Is it an American name?"

I told her Zora is in the Bible.

"In the Bible?"

"Old Testament."

I asked her name.

She said it slowly with a big smile, "Fa-ti-ma. I'm from Algeria." She was gone before I could find out how she happened to be there.

A couple of my book-dealer neighbors helped me set up. Each found a few things he wanted. One handles Civil War materials, the other, ephemera.

"Fugitive works on paper," he explained. "I'd rather have a presidential signature than a bookcase filled with your stuff. Occasional pamphlets, fancy stock certificates, railroad bonds—I'm a specialist in railroad bonds." He showed me a stack of labels from the inside of cigar-box lids and a portfolio of California fruit-box labels. There were movie posters, broadsides, matchbooks too. I asked him why no baseball cards, no comic books? "Too many counterfeits with color Xerox so cheap." He pulled out his best piece, a $5,000 certificate authorizing a Rhode Island privateer to take British prizes during the Revolutionary War.

"Ephemera" bought a few copies of my chapbooks. "Civil War" took my odd volume of Lincoln papers. Both passed over Benjamin Franklin. "Ephemera" gave it as a bookseller's rule that odd volumes and broken sets don't sell. Twelve dollars the first fifteen minutes.

Scouting around a little I noticed that most of my competitors specialize in something: children's books, railroads, sports, miniatures, illustrated books, cookery, Victorian embossed covers, and two for war (in addition to Civil War). No one has a sign up for poetry. I'm the only generalist. I'm by far the cheapest, but I got some frowns from other dealers when they learned that I cannot afford to give a dealer's discount or take checks.

Off to my right folks are selling food. There's a retired couple selling their own jams, tastes offered on twigs they've whittled into little paddles. I bought their plum but passed up some others because they won't swap their groceries for mine. There's a cluster of bread stands next to sheepskin fashions, a stand for hot soups. Someone is running a juicer off a portable generator (orange, celery, carrot, beet—individually or mixed) next to big flat baskets bright with mittens, mufflers, sweaters, and hats. There's a fudge stand with a bronze pot on a gas stove. Then reeks of cheese and the sudden, sharp smell of coffee. I bought a lump of cheese for Jefe. The food people have clusters of benches around like we do. Business is good.

There's a long-limbed, curly-haired boy playing a concertina. His music drifts around like whiffs of food. Little ones sidle over shyly to where he's playing and start bobbing around.

Back to my stand, past "Civil War" and "Ephemera," armed with coffees, jam, and breakfast rolls for my companions. "Civil War" has a clever rig of wooden compartments he piles up to form a rough-and-ready bookcase. He doesn't have to unpack at all, just lifts the lids off his travel boxes, turns them on their sides and latches the lids to the back to get them out of the way and incidentally secure the stack. He can display a lot.

I'm spread out flat on the big sheet of plywood the fair organizers provided, swagged in a bright blue and black African fabric I got offers for all day. The rest of my books were sitting below in shallow boxes, faced out, until an official came by to check my receipt and said that displaying goods in boxes wasn't permitted "for aesthetic reasons." Okay. I rowed them spines up naked on the pavement. Jefe kept safe under the table.

I settled down to a second breakfast feeling tidy and compact at my table. I knew what I had and I'd flagged good things in many. As I lined up books on the ground I happened upon *New England Puritans*, an anthology of New England writing. I riffled the pages. Most of the stuff is pretty heavy going, sermons, sinners fried like spiders over hellfire.

But I came upon a letter Roger Williams wrote to one Major John Mason in 1670: *"Alas! Sir, in calm midnight thoughts, what are these leaves and flowers, and smoke and shadows and dreams of earthly nothings, about which we poor fools and children, as David saith, disquiet ourselves in vain? Alas! what is all the scuffing of this world for, but 'Come, will you smoke it?' What are the contentions and wars of this world about, generally, but for greater dishes and bowls of porridge."*

My first customer was a brisk, tweed-suited old lady with a pile of coiled white hair and fine black-stockinged legs. She said she represented the American Association of University Women and would be glad to collect for their book sale anything I had left at the end of the day.

I offered some things she ought to pick up now, for a price, to ornament her sale. Showed her the Franklin and Roger Williams letters. She then looked over my stock with a bird's cold eye.

Before she moved on to offer her mortuary services to my brothers I learned that her name is Miss Wells and she's a native. But something doesn't fit: there's something Southern in her talking. As she left she mentioned that Babcock's house is not a mile away, a museum now.

There were little spurts and flickers of business until early afternoon—the start of a visit with a tall slight fellow in black leather pants. He had a gaunt face and remarkably long fingers. When he bought my Maeterlinck he seemed to scold that I had odd, old-fashioned tastes. He was maybe thirty but he spoke with such a languid, weary authority I took him for an Edwardian. I set out to explain that my Aunt Helene had put me on to *The Blue Bird of Happiness* because the Swiss woman she taught with had named the school she'd founded the Blue Bird School. But halfway through my Oscar Wilde glazed over and drifted off.

2:00 P.M.: A few desultory callers, no buyers. I left things in care of "Ephemera" and took Jefe for a stroll. Then back to my chair, thinking how blissful it would be to lie down flat and snooze for a few minutes. That cold swim, for all its virtue, had knocked me out. Maybe I closed my eyes.

"I'll swap you lunch for those letters." It was Miss Wells, carrying a basket.

It was $12 worth of books I'd given $5 for, but I was hungry and there was something winsome about her. She wasn't all granite. So, "Sure!" A thermos of black coffee, two peanut-butter-and-jellies wrapped in well-used wax paper she deftly retrieved and smoothed for another day, a peach, a whole ripe tomato—"Just picked it!"—with a pinch of salt screwed into a paper. For Jefe, a bone that had recently been through a soup. He sneezed with pleasure. But not for the bone. He has an extraordinary affection for peanut butter.

I asked her how it was she had a touch of the South in her talking. She laughed a pretty laugh and said there isn't, but a great-grandfather was a lawyer in Charleston. He went off to the Civil War, came back ragged and penniless, "Didn't even have buttons on his coat." Before the war he'd done some legal work for a Westerly cotton broker. The Yankee showed up again in Charleston after things cooled off. He looked up his friend, said "I still owe you for some work you did," and paid him $100 in gold.

That was enough to provide for a family, buy the home the family still owns on Charleston's Battery, and start a fortune. The Charleston lawyer married one of the Westerly man's sisters. "There's been some going back and forth ever since," Miss Wells allowed.

She wanted to talk about the book business. "How much do you make in a day? Do you sell the same things over and over? What sells the best?"

I explained that on days when I set up I take in about $100, but that's not what I make.

"If I take in $100, I may make $25 after expenses and what I paid for the books. As for what sells, it's never the same, even at the same place. A dealer's buying can throw off my idea of a town's tastes. As for what sells best—children's books. When I started this I'd carry the odd Beatrix Potter and *Kim* and *Treasure Island*. My partner kept after me to carry *Alice in Wonderland*. When he learned I hadn't read it he questioned me closely about what children's books I did know and found me so ignorant he made up a list of 'must carry' titles. Tintins are high on it."

I showed her my want list, "But the truth is, most of what I put out is new to me. I keep coming upon new classics." I read to her from something I'd just come upon. It was Sean O'Faolain's autobiography, *Vive Moi!*, a page about one of his grade-school teachers in Cork they'd called "old Doggy," and this about his Auntie Nan, "*a slattern old woman, her hair streeling, her eyes filled with tears, her hands speckled with the dried flecks of the meal she had just been feeding to the hens.*" "There's a lot of politics in it, too. The best books are rooted in place and politics."

Miss Wells asked me to send the O'Faolain on when I finished. It came out that she'd bicycled around Ireland with a classmate after they graduated from Smith sixty years ago. When they got to the Vale of Avoca, her companion discovered the weavers there and decided to set up a business exporting fabric to America.

Peanut butter and jelly sandwiches washed down with black coffee are reviving. I asked Miss Wells if she'd be my audience for a poetry reading. I explained that if nobody reads poetry out loud, performs it, we'll all forget what wonderful things are in these books. I described what Tom does. She said okay.

I walked over to the van, grabbed a sun hat and my brightest Indian bedspread, wrapped myself in the red cloth like a toga, donned the hat, came back to my table and picked up Emily Dickinson. With the fullest voice and gesture I could muster I began declaiming to everyone in particular like an actor to a cold audience, "*I'm nobody / Who are you? / Are you a nobody too? / Then there's a pair of us / Don't tell / They'd banish us you know.*"

At first folks close by started to move away. Jefe gave a surprised bark. But a few gathered closer once they realized it was a show. "*How ugly to be somebody / How public like a frog / To tell your name the livelong day / To an admiring bog!*" I held out the opened book like Tom does as I kept reciting. I sold it before my memorized stock of E.D. lines ran out. By then I'd gotten a little buzz going so I pulled an extra bench over and gave them one of my favorites, Thomas

Hardy's "Phantom Horsewoman." I think I had it sold even
before I came to its haunting end:

> *And though, toil-tired,*
> *He withers daily,*
> *Time touches her not,*
> *But she still rides gaily*
> *In his rapt thought*
> *On that shagged and shaly*
> *Atlantic spot,*
> *And as when first eyed*
> *Draws rein and sings to the swing of the tide.*

For the next hour or so, while Miss Wells took the money
and made change, I stood in front of my stand reading aloud
and talking up my stuff. I got caught up in it. It was fun, and I
could tell that the people on my benches and standing around
were having a good time, too. They loved Dylan Thomas, did-
n't want me to stop reading him. I told them Tom's description of the rapture he felt the first time he read Thomas, "the
transport, exaltation there was complete and immediate. That
kind of beatitude." I sang them the randy Widow's song from
Under Milkwood, "Come and sweep my chimney!" and sold
that too. *Big Sur* went, an odd volume of Thoreau's *Journal*. I
was only twenty lines into William Carlos Williams's
Patterson, Book Two before somebody reached for it.

Cort appeared and sat down on the bench for a bit of my
hucksering. I showed him the American Dream books I'd
picked out for him: Edward Dahlberg's *Because I Was Flesh*,
Wright Morris's *Will's Boy*, and Saul Bellow's *The
Adventures of Augie March*. "These are boys maybe like the
boy you were—their coming of age. Their dreams are in their
stories. How they made their way. How they liked what they
got." And I tried a long shot, the only how-to-live book I've
ever carried, Helen and Scott Nearing's *Living the Good Life*.

There's a lot of good dreaming in their telling how they came to build stone houses by hand and do their daily living. "I visited the Nearings once," I told Cort. "Showed up unannounced at their Maine farm. Scott was in his nineties, tanned and tough. He was fertilizing apple trees when we arrived, showed us his mulch and compost piles, gave us his July 4th address about how America was managing with the oldest government in the world. He asked if our freedom protects us from inflation, taxation, and unemployment. When I met his wife, Helen, I told her I'd read their book. She asked how it had changed my life. I said it had given me some ideas for the future. 'What about now?' she wanted to know."

The crowd had pretty well thinned out by 4:00 P.M. and a steady breeze was sending fountain spray over my wares, so I quit. Cort and Miss Wells helped me pack up. We counted the day's takings. Things rounded out to $115. Not a break-even day, I explained to Miss Wells. "I paid $40 for what I sold; the fair fee was $50; and I have to count something for gas and oil for four hundred miles. I'm out about $50 for a night on the ocean and a day's living." We all agreed that it's okay to go that much out-of-pocket for a good everyday. And, whatever the religion, some good gospel got out.

Miss Wells insisted we visit Dr. Babcock's house. Cort hadn't seen it either, so he drove us over. Left Jefe outside to investigate the lilacs. It's a modest white-frame place facing the road, a sort of carved bonnet over the front door, the interior a small graceful space with tall windows nearly to the floor. Light poured in laced with tree shadows. The place has the elegance of a brief Bach air. The doctor risked a lot to make a new government here based on new principles.

I invited my new friends to the beer garden for supper. It was too early for dinner for them, or they were too polite to accept my offer, but they sat with me while I had mine. The waitress again honored Jefe with a bouquet of scraps. She said she has a dog too, makes up these plates for him, there's always plenty.

As we got ready to leave Cort said we could stay with him the next time we come over, or at least park Zora in his driveway and use the shower. Miss Wells promised to look for a yard we could use. Since I'm not a charity I can't have a stand when her university women set up at the high school. The difference seems to be that my bookselling is not profitable while hers is not-for-profit. I told her I'm going to reorganize as a foundation. Then I'll be able to set up in parks and school yards, solicit gifts, and award myself grants.

Dinner and two strong coffees helped but I was worn out. It hurt to drive, my head, legs, shoulders, back all complaining. When we got back to Hatfield I slept for fourteen hours.

> *When I was young,*
> *I had not given a penny for a song*
> *Did not the poet sing it with such airs*
> *That one believed he had a sword upstairs.*

> —W.B. Yeats
> *The Green Helmut and Other Poems*

CHAPTER 11

Labor Day Weekend

Friday afternoon driving up to Brattleboro, Winesap apples and a chunk of cheddar in my pockets. As my neighbor Freddy says, "They go down together kinda easy." I catch myself singing despite the hurricane skies and how blowy it is. It may rain. Zora gets pushed around a lot by these winds. One day last winter, just about here, a gust hit us midship. The road was icy, the van was empty. With hardly a bump we glided into a cornfield and sent up a crowd of crows. Then silence. I let most of the air out of the tires and crunched back onto the road.

This promises to be our biggest weekend if the weather clears. People are in good spirits here over Labor Day, almost a Mardi Gras feeling, easy merriment before school starts and the first frost.

So a heavy load again, layers of book boxes, then boards, sign, sawhorses, then more boxes piled in among the sawhorse legs. Not a tight load, I discovered, as we rounded the exit curve at Brattleboro. There was a crashing sound as cartons slid and tipped. Jefe barked alarm as Pound's *ABC of Reading* caromed into his box. I pulled over and petted him, said I was sorry. He licked my hand, but, ever since, when we set out he checks to see how high the load is piled. Too high and he squeezes into the doorwell.

It did rain but it let up by Saturday noon. By 1:00 I had the sign out and a table set up. Jefe was in his box, wrapped against

the damp in an old coat. I spread out an old rug with a bedspread
on top against the wet and laid out some children's books from
Tom's "must carry" list: *The Three Musketeers, Alice in
Wonderland*, Vachel Lindsay's poems for children (one line I
glanced upon, *"And the ponies danced on silver feet"*).
When children show up I point them to their special place
and they flop right down. I did too after setting up that first
table. I picked up *The Crystal Cabinet*, "an anthology of
poetry for children," and I'm the child they had in mind:
*"Come and kiss me sweet and twenty / youth's a stuff 'twill not
endure"* and *"Sing we for love and idleness, / Naught else is
worth the having."*
    My first callers were two pretty kids, the boy and girl both
slight and tanned, skimpy clothes, her small breasts high and
pointing. Each is wearing one gold earring like a gypsy. The
gold glows against their tan skin. Maybe they *are* gypsies. He
has his first beard. Right away she picked up *Bread and
Puppet Theater*. What a spur to setting up more when I see
them going over the one table I've got ready.
    The lad found something on stone-house construction. I was
now pouring out titles on the neighboring tables, but that was it.
    They came over to pay. "Do you go to school around here?"
    "We were at Marlboro," she said, "but it's $25,000 a year
and we don't want to take on any more loans." They're trans-
ferring to the community college for one-tenth the tuition.
They'll be on their own for room and board. What about their
friends? The girl explained that they're joining a commune
where they'll exchange labor for shelter, firewood, and vegetables. He's a carpenter, she has a computer. "It's even better
than college, people of all ages." She hopes they can manage
a year together on $9,500.
    Their books came to $5. That covered my permit but I'm
not yet eating on my earnings. They brought me luck though,

drew others, got a hubbub going. Tom arrived, the sun came out, and Jefe lay toasting.

Tom had to get us the permit. The selectmen want to discourage yard sales that occupy the same yard and circulate the same goods weekend after weekend. They worry about a trashy town image and too much traffic. They miss the point. Most people driving through town on Saturdays enjoy these sales, like to stop, visit, paw some well-pawed goods, pass on bits of money for something they'll use or admire for a spell with the happy knowledge that it's worth three, maybe ten times what they gave.

We now display the blue paper as required. We can get only three a year. We'd like to stop here five times, so I've put out a petition to the effect that as a free school and public utility we enhance the town and should be encouraged. Customers are invited to sign. My two pretty kids did.

The lady who owns this yard drove by. Since she won't take any money for rent, I try to give her books. I waved and got her to stop. She wouldn't claim her "totin' rights" last year. Her son had just died. She told me he'd "gone to the light." She's recovered a little now, picked up books about water—Annie Dillard's *Pilgrim at Tinker Creek*, Mark Twain's *Life on the Mississippi*—said her boy told her in a dream to move to a place by water, so she has. She gave me a hug when she left, made me glad.

A handsome, dark-eyed lad came up, his right hand wrapped in a cloth cast. "Bow too hard?" Tom asked. "I *am* a musician!" the young man answered, laughing. "I play the Irish drum. Injured my hand playing too long in Kyoto at an Irish pub called Murphy's."

"Wow!" said Tom, brightening up for a good talk. The young man's name is John. He's a graduate student at Santa Barbara, just returned from visiting Japan on a grant to study

Zen Buddhism. He asked Tom his age, wanted to know how
he keeps so fit.

"No red meat and vitamin C."

He'd picked up our illustrated *Decameron*. Tom asked him
if he knew what it was.

"A collection of romantic tales."

"Something like that, but do you know what occasioned
their telling? Like the *Arabian Nights* and *Canterbury Tales*,
there's a story behind the story-telling."

Tom read from an early page: "*Such was the cruelty of
Heaven, and perhaps in part of men, that between March and
July [1348] more than one hundred thousand persons died
within the walls of Florence, what between the violence of the
plague and the abandonment in which the sick were left by the
cowardice of the healthy. And before the plague it was not
thought that the whole city held so many people.*"

"Picture this," Tom continued, mixing the telling and
reading aloud that is his style, "seven beautiful young
women '*educated and of noble blood, fair to look upon,
well-mannered and of graceful modesty,*' all related by ties
of blood, friendship or neighborship, and all now without
family. They meet in church one Tuesday morning. One of
them proposes that they flee to a country house. As they plan
their flight they are joined by three young men, lovers whose
love could not be quenched or even cooled by the horror of
the times, the loss of relatives and friends, or even fear for
themselves.

"They go off with servants to a fine, well-ordered villa.
They agree that each should rule for a day. The first to rule
announces, '*As you see, the sun is high and the heat great,
and nothing can be heard but the cicadas in the olive trees.
To walk about at this hour would be foolish. Here it is cool
and lovely, and, as you see, there are games of chess and*

draughts which everyone can amuse himself with, as he chooses. But, if my opinion is followed, we shall not play games, because in games the mind of one of the players must necessarily be distressed without any great pleasure to the other player or the onlookers. Let us rather spend this hot part of the day in telling tales, for thus one person can give pleasure to the whole company. When each of us has told a story, the sun will be going down and the heat less, and we can then go walking anywhere we choose for our amusement.'

"And so, ten tales a day for ten days, and we have *The Decameron.*"

Several people had gathered to listen and to look at the book. We could have sold five. But I wondered what happened among those chaste maidens and their lovers after they'd heard those heated tales. And at the end of the tenth day, what then? I was too bustling and hurried to ask Tom about the ever after.

Four tables going now, each one bright with a cut-down plastic milk jug stuffed with black-eyed susans. Mary brought them by on her way to the Farmers' Market. The rain kept everyone in all morning, now the sun is bringing them all out. Folks drive down from the Farmers' Market munching their late lunches. Such a one came up to me with a tight little smile. "I'm a lawyer. What do you have in the way of law books?" He's round like a keg of good German beer, richly turned out. His eyes don't track, one wambles to the left while he fixes you hard with the other. His remaining hair is a monk's fringe around his ears.

I showed him one of my favorites, Reginald Hine's *Confessions of an Uncommon Attorney*, an antiquarian's omnium gatherum of law matters and lawyers, compiled by an English estates practitioner: bits from sixteenth century wills and pleadings he found in his firm's attic, things he came upon in old practice books, local church registers, land records.

I opened it to a quote from one Thomas Overbury (1581–1613): *"An Honest Lawyer: A trusty Pilot, a true priest of Justice, one who wears the conscience as well as the gowne, weighs the cause as well as the gold, and knows, but never uses, the nice snapperadoes of Practice."*

My customer fanned a few pages, then laid it aside absently. "What else?" I was surprised; never had anyone spurned Overbury's snapperadoes before. I tried him on the Oliver Wendell Holmes–Sir Frederick Pollock letters.

"Why would I want to read this?"

"There's law in it, but mainly I like it for the heart-tellings of those two aristocrats. Holmes writes about getting shot in the Civil War, readying himself to drink laudanum if the pain got too great, wondering if he'd ever get his 'chance at life,' as he put it, how grateful he was for having had it."

I showed him a letter Holmes wrote Pollock in 1891: *"This month I have passed the equator of fifty. Life grows more equable as one grows older; not less interesting, but I hope a little more impersonal. An old man ought to be sad. I don't know whether I shall be when the wind is west and the sky clear."*

My lawyer wagged his head no. "Those aren't law books, they're books about life. You're a philosopher."

Holmes went off later that day in the hands of a bristle-haired, bow-tied, gruff old bulldog of a history professor. We didn't talk until he came over to pay. I tried him on Hine's *Confessions*. He already had it. Then I showed him *Simple Justice*, an account of the school desegregation cases. He had that too, but those two friends in common confirmed our agreement on *"certain ultimata of belief,"* as the Autocrat of the Breakfast Table put it.

He told me about his surprise on returning from World War II and encountering the Jim Crow laws for the first time. He'd grown up around Philadelphia and was amazed when a train conductor told him he couldn't sit in the last car of the trolley from Baltimore to Ruxton because that was for blacks.

A year later, he went to teach at William & Mary College. One afternoon he noticed a black man studying on the lawn under an open classroom window. A few days later it was raining and he encountered the same man sitting in the hall outside an open classroom door. He went up to him. "Look, if you want a place to study, there's an empty classroom. . . ." The man explained that he was a law student; although Virginia law forbade his taking classes "in" the college, if he wanted to hang around outside and overhear, that was okay.

Tom came back from the Farmers' Market beaming, loaded down with coffees, hot stuffed pitas, and a clutch of fruit tarts all just remaindered—"four bucks, the lot!" The Market people go home at 3:00.

The professor sat down to snack with us. His name is Kit. He's on vacation. He'd been to the market too and asked why we don't set up there.

"I applied once," I told him. "Got turned down because our books aren't handmade. Maybe we could sell our chapbooks, but not my usual stock." I described the better arrangement at the Westerly Crafts Fair.

Amazing how one name can set fire to a conversation. Today it was Churchill: what a leader he was, what a presence, what a wit. Tom told about Churchill's mildly insulting the lady next to him at a dinner party. "Winston! You are drunk," she exclaimed. "Yes, Madam," he rumbled, "but you are ugly, and I shall be sober tomorrow."

People gathered around as Kit gave us the story of Churchill going to an Old Boys' Day at Harrow when he was in his dotage. He was not expected to speak, he was too old, too feeble for that. He came in slowly, a huge old worn-down mountain of a man. He was introduced. He was expected to acknowledge the applause with a wave and sit down. He remained standing. More applause. Still he stood. The place hushed. "I have learned one thing in life," he said very slowly, "Never give up. Never. Never. Never. Never. Never. Never give up!"

Someone told how Churchill arranged his own funeral, had the startled congregation at St. Paul's sing "The Battle Hymn of the Republic" and his body ferried up the Thames. One thing he didn't plan: As his funeral barge passed upriver the operators dipped the beaks of their huge wharf-side cranes and blew their horns in his honor.

"Churchill was known to cry," Kit said. "His was the last generation when it was not unmanly to shed tears."

Where do we get our books, Kit wanted to know. He's on his way to Cape Cod, told us about the Wellfleet Library Sale that begins on Labor Day. He's gone to it for years. Lots of good bargains. He described the string of used-book stores along the old road up to Wellfleet. I've never been on the Cape. I said I'd like to come over for that library sale, hadn't planned to set up on Labor Day anyway. He gave me a number to call. He's rented a house for a couple of weeks.

A lull after Kit left, time to read around in our titles. I usually borrow back some things I see in a new light when they're on our tables. Compensation for titles I've pulled from my home shelves.

A girl came by and selected a wonderful Willa Cather, *My Antonia*. That sent me off on a hunt around our tables for our other Willa Cather titles. Tom meanwhile was off on a browse of his own. He pulled out Josephine Tey's *The Daughter of*

Time. "One of the best books ever written," he exclaimed. I thought I'd take it for a long winter night, but a boy who'd overheard him reached for it.

A little later I had a scare. Tom had just gone home for a nap when a lean man in a military outfit drove up in an official-looking car with whip antennas and radios crackling. At first I thought he was a town official out to check our permit. He was sallow-faced, maybe forty. Left the engine running as he got out and lit a cigarette.

He wore a thick black belt with a leather case on one hip and a pistol on the other. Black boots very shiny. But there was no particular insignia on his car or uniform. Now I took him for one of our new patriots.

He started talking loudly to everyone around about his daughter. The other customers moved away uneasily. I was frightened and embarrassed, circled to the other side of the van and sat down by my tree with a book, hoping he'd go away. He followed, still talking about his daughter. She's hopelessly, recklessly pursuing an older married man, making a fool of herself, risking her job. "What books do you have about that? What books to help her? What books to help him?"

He found *Women Who Love Too Much.* "That's it," he said. "That's her to a T." His hands were shaking. It turned out he didn't have any money but somebody up the road owed him a buck and he'd be back. I told him to take the book along. He did, and he came back and paid for it.

"Thanks," he said, handing me the dollar. He wasn't shaking any more, seemed oddly meek. I wonder if he knew he'd made me sweat.

Dusk. Sharply cooler. A little woodsmoke in the air. Tom came back to help me pack up. We were starting work when a neighbor of Tom's came by, a literary agent, quite a handsome man once, tall and thick, long graying hair combed back, a fine houndstooth jacket, yellow ascot, cigar, a port-wine voice. He said our offerings were pretty good, "But there's no system to the way you show them," pointing to Rabelais guffawing away next to a book on mountaineering, and that right next to *The Oxford Book of Hymns.* "Why do you carry what you carry?"

He bought the three books he'd pointed to. I asked him if he'd bought *Two Mountains and a River* because of what I'd flagged in it: *"The worst part of a war, as many of us are beginning to realize, is the end."*

"Yes. Very seductive. It was Voltaire, I think, who, when old, said he could still win the favors of a fair woman if he could talk to her alone. Once she heard him, he said, she would forget his face and her indifference. That seems to be the way you're selling books."

He made a second pass and gathered up some Laurie Lee titles. I asked him what sort of books he's interested in. He laughed, "I wouldn't want to pin myself down, but I know what sort of books interest you."

With that it came to a $118 day. Tom and I hauled up the heavy sign together, jumbled our books into the van, and left our tables standing out, pretty sure that no one would make off with them. We hid the sign in the nearby woods. Fifty degrees when we left.

Sunday dawned bright blue. We finished setting up just as the church across the way let out with the jubilant clanks of a good, dry Yankee bell.

Our first caller was a church lady, crinkly-faced and friendly. "You got nice books, but I'm looking for something really empty to get lost in, a Harlequin. You don't have any Harlequins do you? I handed her Anaïs Nin's *Delta of Venus*: "Same idea only a lot more exciting. $1.75." She read a few pages and jammed it into her purse. "That oughta do it," she said smiling as she paid. "I'll remember your book truck."

Our Central Vermont Railroad man from Memorial Day stopped by. He said he wanted garden books this time, something to fill in until the seed and plant catalogs start showing up. He said perennials are really his passion, but he's still reading the "women and old poets" his wife is studying. I asked him how he's doing with the Montaigne he bought the last time. "Keeps me ahead of her," he said. "I never showed her that one. I memorize parts and let them out sometimes when she gets going." He went off today with Thomas Jefferson's *Garden Book*.

Someone picked up *Drinking with Dickens*. Tom called over to her, "Did you hear about Dickens's trip to America? He went into a bar and asked for a martini. Bartender asked him, 'Olive or twist?'" The folks around liked that.

Quiet for a long time. We picnicked on some sandwiches Martha had sent along, then Tom settled down to work the *Times* crossword. He's sure enough to do it in ink. I tinkered with the van's motor. The generator is going. Zora is showing her age. She's rusting out. The last time I took her in for a state inspection the garage man showed me where her frame's one-third gone in front. "Don't take any big bumps," he laughed as I drove off. "She'll go down like a turtle." He said he wouldn't pass her again. I thought about the loads she hauls at seventy and the bumpy Vermont dirt roads we travel. I guess I've been going a few miles on that famed German over-engineering.

A good thing *I* don't have to pass any inspection to set out. My driver's license has five years in it before they even check my eyes again. And my frame? I could turn turtle anytime too. Funny how things run together. In my browse around earlier I came upon something in one of Emerson's *Journals*, "*Thoughts of the turtle are all turtle.*"

A couple arrived and started picking over our tables very carefully, piling up books. I cleaned up a little and asked what they were interested in. "Books about England and New England." They're dealers. They found a lot. As I brought them boxes to fill I began to feel foolish. I'd marked my stuff too cheap, I was too anxious to sell. They pawed but left my well-used *Practical Cogitator*. As they drove away I rushed it to safety.

At times like this I'm torn about what I'm doing. Why can't I rejoice in that big sale? It came to $90. The people were nice. But they weren't buying books, they were buying stock, and it's not the wholesaling of potatoes that I'm after. Like a good waiter I delight in putting people onto good things, pleasuring in their pleasure and pleased with their tip. But I don't intend they should empty the pot.

I hold out to the world that I'm a book dealer pushing books, that's my work. The more buying and selling the better. Some days, when I look at my mountain of boxes and consider the state of my wallet, I mark good things down just to make sales. But most of the time I'm more a fisherman than a merchant. I want company, not cash. But if I don't get some cash when I bait my hooks will I have courage enough to go out again?

I worry about the luxury of my part-time occupation. I don't have to live on it any more than my great-aunt Zora depended on her style-shop takings for her oatmeal, so is it really work? Is it still work if you draw only part of your living from it? Is it work if you draw your pleasure from it? Zora's shop didn't make money but it gave her a life. How do you count that? Maybe it comes to how you lie down at night and how you rise in the morning. Sleep is a boon. One test of work is the sleep that rewards it.

The Practical Cogitator: Some titles take you easily enough, but some are off-putting. This one has a musty, oldcodgerish air about it. As a dealer in used books I am largely a dealer in old books, things out of fashion. This one is a commonplace book compiled by two Boston editors from 1943 to 1944, probably with troops in mind, something compact to reach a wide range of interests. But before most of us would pick it up today we'd have to be shown how frisky and bold those editors were, how broad their range, and the fun they had in making their compilation.

Here is Edward Coke (1532–1634): *"Let us now peruse our ancient authors, for out of the old fields must come the new corn."* And John Selden (1584–1654) on justice: *"We see the judges look like lions, but we do not see who moves them."* The index alone is forty pages of sources and subjects. It sold for $3 in 1945. I got it for 50¢, ex-library, shaken and worn.

Who is compiling commonplace books today? It takes wide reading and a lot of time. Most readers now are specialists and rushed at that. I put out a small chapbook every year, twenty-five pages of quotes from books in the van, "He Said, She Said, They Wrote." I give a definition on the first page: "This is a chapbook, 'a small book or pamphlet of popular tales, ballads, etc. formerly hawked about by chapmen,' themselves 'hawkers or peddlers.' It is a ransack of things that illuminate life or reveal peculiar darknesses."

With Tom's help I hope to publish a big one in a couple of years. A good commonplace book is like a good party: you encounter some old friends and maybe make some new ones. The difference between a commonplace book and an anthology is the difference between a memoir and an autobiography: the former can be as partial as remembering, selective and arbitrary; the latter is expected to be complete and balanced.

A strong-looking woman with two young children asked for books about mathematics. Playing for time, I pointed her young ones to their special spot.

"No, but we can do astronomy."

"I saw what you have," she said brusquely. "It's all dated. A lot's changed in five years."

"The stars have changed?"

"Yes! We've found some new ones." She explained that she's a math and science teacher, started telling me about space probes, black holes, and quarks. "But the biggest change is how we think about time. Time before time. How we figure the age of the solar system.

"Your books are okay," she said, sensing my dismay. "I run into this problem all the time at schools and public libraries. The books they have—like yours—map the universe as accurately as we mapped the human brain before CAT scans."

I asked her if she knew John Aubrey's *Brief Lives*: "He's got an astronomer in there who anticipated Newton, Robert Hooke. Take a look."

I showed her the place: "*[His] was the greatest Discovery in Nature that ever was since the World's Creation. It never was so much as hinted by any man before. I wish he had writt plainer, and afforded a little more paper.*"

Aubrey's *Lives* found a new home. So did *A Little House on the Prairie*. The astronomy books ended up in a box for Anna Wells's next sale.

Tom was talking with a big, chunky man. Something about Samuel Johnson's recommending Addison as a writer for writers to imitate as he showed our nicely bound and slipcased copy of the *Roger De Coverly Papers*. No sale. The gent wanted a book on Antarctica. We had no Antarctica. Tom trotted out our geographies, then natural histories, the Ice Age, books about glaciers. No. "But my wife will get some books from you. She likes poetry. She'll buy all your poetry books."

"I just like it," she explained when Tom asked if she's after poetry as a student or a teacher. Her name is Debbie. She works the night shift at the Brattleboro Retreat downtown. We scouted out poetry books for her. As they piled up she looked more and more bewildered.

"Would it help if I gave you tastes?" Tom asked. "I can quote from them so you can choose what you like." She nodded. From memory he gave her some lines from Shelley's "To a Skylark," then a Shakespeare sonnet, then one by Edna St. Vincent Millay that knocked my breath out:

> *What lips my lips have kissed, and where, and why,*
> *I have forgotten, and what arms have lain*
> *Under my head till morning; but the rain*
> *Is full of ghosts tonight, that tap and sigh*
> *Upon the glass and listen for reply,*
> *And in my heart there stirs a quiet pain*
> *For unremembered lads that not again*
> *Will turn to me at midnight with a cry.*
> *Thus in the winter stands the lonely tree,*
> *Nor knows what birds have vanished one by one,*
> *Yet knows its boughs more silent than before*:
> *I cannot say what loves have come and gone,*
> *I only know that summer sang in me*
> *A little while, that in me sings no more.*

Three or four people were standing rapt as Tom read and recited Edith Sitwell's "*Still falls the rain,*" something gritty and banging from Carl Sandburg, fragments from *The Greek Anthology*, Gerard Manley Hopkins's "Windhover," some Thomas Hardy.

A lady remarked to another bystander that she'd come by today just on the off-chance "he'd be at it again."

Debbie's bill came to $30—a lot of books at Zora's prices, ten or fifteen. "So much wealth," Tom mused looking at the bag, sorry to see so many of his friends departing but hopeful for their new home.

A doctor showed up asking if I had any more Gertrude Stein. He'd bought all we had Memorial Day weekend, told me today that he'd sent the lot to his stepfather in Australia. "Australia needs what Stein's got," he explained. I understood. But today we were out of Stein. I got him to try John Berryman's *The Dream Songs* instead. He said that if they felt right he'd send those to Perth as well. I said if they didn't I'd give him his money back.

A bag lady visited. Now and then over the summer I'd noticed her walking slowly along our road, bent over, burdened with two bulging plastic bags. She's round, very tan, gold-rim glasses, her cheeks almost copper, her hair scaggled and burnt pale. She's maybe sixty, carries a rubber-tipped stick. She explained to us how cheaply made crutch and cane tips are these days; this one won't last a week. Says she walks from Marlboro to Brattleboro and back every dry day, scouting Route 9 for cans and bottles she can collect the 5¢ deposit on. She makes it to Brattleboro in time for lunch at the Seniors Center. We figured she walks twenty miles, down the mountain in the morning, then back up. She said she picks up pretty things as she goes along, found a necklace once. "But I get stung by bees a lot when I pick up my cans and bottles."

Mary went over to her truck for some of the good bee-sting poultice she carries. She works in gardens and gets stung, too. We told our visitor she could have any book she wanted. She wasn't surprised, took a good hour choosing, went over every table very carefully before selecting Needham on Chinese science. "It has something on acupuncture in it. Statistics. What it works on. It works on me."

Mary gave her a bag of the bee-sting potion, explained about applying the herbs and then, maybe, baking soda. The woman's glasses were bleary. Mary offered to clean them, brought over a clean rag and some water. Then a cup. Our visitor said "Thanks," nodded to us, arranged her skirt, her bags, her stick, and went off slowly.

The day's total came to $215: $373 for the weekend. Maybe a little profit in that, so I'll give myself a holiday. Cape Cod has a magic ring.

> *Best and brightest, come away!*
> *Fairer far than this fair Day,*
> *Which, like thee to those in sorrow,*
> *Comes to bid a sweet good-morrow . . .*

—Percy Bysshe Shelley, "The Invitation"

CHAPTER 12

Cape Cod

Labor Day morning I got up at 4:00 A.M. for a run to the Cape to meet my new friend of a couple of days ago for breakfast and the Wellfleet Library Sale. With a "Stay! Be guard dog," I parked Jefe with Martha. He knew he was missing something good, gave me a reproachful look before slipping under the sofa he visits for sulks and thunderstorms.

Zora started right up. Empty of cargo we brisked along. By 7:00 we were on the old road up the Cape's spine. Passed a big used bookshop called Parnassus, a reformed church or school with honor-system shelves of 50¢ books outside. I didn't have time to shop. I had to meet Kit.

But first I wanted to see the ocean. I drove down a side road through oak scrub to a clearing. The beach was way below me. I slid down through bright-colored sand mixed with cobbles. Fishermen around, no swimmers. A long, curving, empty sweep of sand in both directions. Good booming rollers. I waded in a little. Stinging cold.

I found my landmarks, my friend, and my breakfast. On our way to the library sale, we passed a gray-shingled farmhouse close by the road, a pump out front. Kit said he used to call on an old book scout who'd lived there. The man got started in the book business during the Depression when a friend offered him a few dollars to help clear out a house. At the end only the books remained. The friend said, "You take 'em, Frank. Send 'em to Goodspeed's in Boston and see what

they'll give you." He did. By return mail he got a check for
$50, enough to live on for a couple of months in those days.
So he got into the book business. He kept shop in an outbuild-
ing, sat out front by the pump, barefoot in old clothes. He
liked to tell how he acquired two hundred years of Norwich
town records for free when they remodeled the courthouse
and discarded them as trash. Frank told Kit that the New York
dealers took him for a hick, "Come up here, think I don't
know what I have, but they kept me going for nearly a year on
those town records."

The sale spilled out of a little frame shed behind the library,
books spread out in boxes on the ground outside, the inside
jammed with shelves and boxes, books skied up beyond
reach. Hardbacks priced 50¢ and up, paperbacks and children's a quarter. The hardbacks were mostly fiction and politics, two areas I'm wary of, but I found some children's books
on Tom's list.

The space inside was very tight. Hardly room for two people and more than half of that occupied by the stout mistress
of the proceedings. A certain etiquette was required to slither
and squeeze and snatch the treasure you wanted while not
telegraphing your intentions. We were five in there. The
intense scent of the hunt pervaded. I found Gilbert Highet's
inspired introduction to Roman poetry, *Poets in a Landscape*;
a fairly new thesaurus; and R.H. Blyth's *Haiku*, four volumes
printed in Japan and bound in boards covered with woven
grass.

What with a nice clutch of children's books, some okay
paperbacks, and those other books, I carried off two grocery
bags I paid $4 for.

Over to the bay side for lunch in a falling-down gray shed.
They serve good seafood in the front part; in the back an old
sea dog as tumble-down as his premises sits on a planked-up

dais, lording it over a warren of magazines and jumbled books
on critically sagging shelves. Old boat parts and cap guns are
also displayed. Not much is marked. It's the sea dog's collection. He doesn't really want to sell it.

He told me he makes his main money selling back issues of
magazines: "$20 or $30 for a *Life*. Three or four go outta here
most every week." He confided that one sale he's got coming
up will send him to Florida for the entire winter.

He had some Harvard Classics on a high shelf. I said I'd
like to buy the lot, asked the price. "Can't get 'em no more.
Over. Done. Kaput. Used to get 'em. Not any more. Museum
things. Savin' 'em for a museum."

Kit drove me over to Nauset Marsh and the fringe of shore
where Henry Beston spent a winter alone in a borrowed cabin,
the Outermost House. He made a fine book of his time there.
The cabin was blown away in a hurricane a few years ago.

Thoreau walked along here, wrote in his diary, "*All of
America is at my back.*" His *Cape Cod* sits next to *Outermost
House* on our tables when we have them both and are orga-
nized enough to know it. I try to anchor Gavin Maxwell's
Ring of Bright Water, the tale of his years alone on the Isle of
Soway in the Hebrides in that group too. You hear and feel
and taste the sea in those books—become one with the man
facing it.

Before I headed back Kit and I had a late afternoon coffee
together. Kit talked about driving an ambulance for the
American Field Service during World War II. For a while, his
ambulance was assigned to the English Eighth, "a singing
Army, mostly American Civil War songs, 'Tenting Tonight.'"
He said that after the New Zealanders were decimated at
Monte Cassino the replacement Aussies and English stood on
either side of the road at midnight and serenaded the survivors
with the Maori hymn, "*Now is the hour / When we must say*

good-bye." Of another day: "As the Jerries shelled our position, the officers at senior mess discussed the women in Thackery."

I asked him about titles I ought to carry. He said he'd have to think on that. But then he mentioned three: Steven Vincent Benét's *John Brown's Body*; John Bunyan's *Pilgrim's Progress*; and *The Journal of the Lewis & Clark Expedition.*

Driving out I passed a sign to a public beach. I gave myself a twenty-minute detour. Drove to the parking area, changed in the bathhouse, ran at the water like a tackle. It tackled me. I couldn't get my breath. Lurched out. Showered in cold water warmer than that seawater, then back on my way—fifteen minutes.

On my way home, I stopped at Parnassus and found a copy of *Pilgrim's Progress: "Fulness to such a burden is / That go on pilgrimage."*

CHAPTER 13

Columbus Day

Thinking I needed some hungrier venues for Zora (looked up venue—"a coming on, in order to strike"—exactly!), I was nosing around southern New Hampshire looking for a place to set up. I came across "BOOKS" painted on a tall narrow house, siding flaking away, a strip of flowers out front, a painting of three large, fading strawberries hanging on the wall by the basement door with another sign: "This is a Self-Service Shop. The light switch is on your right. Have a good time. Turn out the light when you leave."

Why did I feel so tickled to be let into this place on my own recognizance, on my honor (dubious as it is, God knows), alone and musing in a richly musty, sag-ceilinged, damp, dirt-floored room? Books were a dollar apiece, three for $2—Hawthorne, politics, the swelled and weathered fictions of thirty years ago, a lot of good children's books honorably retired from the Boston Public Library, Penguin thrillers, a run of recent lurid-covered paperback crime/scandal/bodice-rippers no better than they should be.

I was lost in titles when I heard approaching a big humming purring sound like an enormous bumblebee, a sweet noise, not threatening. A large reddish shape in a surround of boozy fumes hove through the doorway. She saw me, hauled up, then giggled deeply.

"Aaah, you've caught me talkin' to myself!"

"That's okay. I do it, too. Is this your shop?"

"It's my shop," she said slowly, thickly, in broad Yankee. She had some side teeth missing. "Don't spend much time in it accounta the damp."

"What's it called?"

"Books!" she said emphatically. She'd set her feet apart as if braced against a strong wind. She has a large, moist face, pretty, tan over florid, small blurred eyes, straying dark to gray hair reefed down under a dark rose cloth. She's bulky in a smudged dark-blue skirt and a worn tartan jacket.

"No need for any more of a name," she laughed. "Fellow up the road just opened a grocery store. Calls it John's Variety. 'Variety what?' I asked him. What's the variety in groceries?"

For all she's firmly anchored she's weaving a little on her own tide. I like her whisky fragrance. Why is it so comforting? It used to scare me when I smelled liquor on my father.

"Bet you've got more variety than John has."

"Ah, yer a darlin'," she said, as she lurched over to give me a hug of greeting.

"What's your name?" I asked.

"Louise. Louise Burke. Mrs. Louise Burke. Married fifteen years. Divorced. Marriage is like a bad job. No benefits. And then you're fired. But I got two good kids, and I lived pretty grand up there"—she waved vaguely. "Now I'm down here. On the corner. 'I'd live in a house by the side of the road and be a friend to man.' I have good neighbors. They'd pick me up if they found me lookin' dead in the yard."

She wanted to know my name, what I did. I pointed to the bus and told her a little about Zora. She nodded slowly, ruminatively, sizing me up.

"What did you do before you took up bookselling?" I asked.

"Schoolteaching. I could teach a stone to read. I like reading, being around books, anthropology. Isn't anthropology *something?*"

She hadn't moved from her anchorage so I asked her about a title I'm looking for, H.F.M. Prescott's *The Man on a Donkey.*

"What's it about?"

"It's a chronicle of thirty years of Henry VIII's reign, life in a small nunnery in the north of England, the North Country Rebellion to save the Roman Church."

"The religious give me books to sell," she said. "They're over there in the corner—Christian Science, bibles. A lot of people just *give* me books."

"Me, too. People who are moving. They know they're valuable but they don't want to sell them. Part of your life is in a book you've read. Selling it doesn't feel right. It deserves to be put in friendly hands. And maybe they just want to help us along."

She nodded gravely. "We're priests," she said. "Now tell me about *The Man on a Donkey.*"

Historical fiction. A friend put me onto it. I went hiking in Wales, passed ruined abbey after ruined abbey—Tintern, Llanthony, Abbey Dore. I began to wonder what became of all the books, the teachers, the medicine, the music, the bells. Why did the people let Henry get away with it? At Christmas, what did they think? When their babies came and when they were dying—what did they think? The silence struck me more than anything. All the music and chants, the murmur of prayers—gone. *The Man on a Donkey* is about that time, the story of a small abbey in Yorkshire and the storms that broke it.

"There's Henry, gross and gorgeous in velvet the color of flame, the herb-strewn floors of court, Thomas Cromwell skulking about soft in dark velvet slippers, the rebels' one-eyed 'Great Captain' Robert Aske, the sounds and smells of spring in the North, the muzzle of the priory mule 'soft as a night-moth,' the color of new beech leaves. It's a beautiful and gripping thing, and long! Seven hundred pages. It takes you into that world, that time."

Louise stared at me through a long pause.

"No, it isn't here."

To brighten things I asked her about the pin on her jacket and the stones she wore.

"Diamonds," she said briskly. "Diamonds are cheap now. Look!" She held out her hands, wrists and fingers heavy with bracelets and rings. "Makes me feel rich. Sometimes when people die you want to take on what gives power to their memory. These are all *inherited*."

Suddenly she shook herself like a large animal waking up. "Have fun. The light is there for when you go."

It was cold and empty in there after she left. The place felt small, dank. I was up to one book shy of $20 worth when I found the *Super Tramp*.

Now, the day before I found myself here I'd been leafing through George Allen's catalog. I like going through book catalogs, ticking off things I'd like to own. They charm me just as they charmed Flannery O'Connor, who once wrote a friend, "I get lists from _____. I am like the little boy who just liked to *feel* candy. I like to read booklists."

In George's catalog I'd hit on the entry for W.H. Davies's *The Autobiography of a Super Tramp*. The title caught my eye. I fancy tramps and tramping, so the picture of a Super Tramp worked on me powerfully. But $30 was too much, even for such a pleasure as might last the time of turning three hundred pages. And suddenly, happily, here it is, one of the pocket blues in the English Travellers Library.

Louise's wooden cash box is a small slant-top affair overwhelmed by its large padlock. A note was taped to the top: "Make checks out to _____. Please have a fine, fine time!!"

Someone had written on one side, "Louise, your shop is one of the most wonderful in the world. I come by a lot. Thank you so much. Sam."

I bought the tramp book and a thesaurus for myself and twenty-eight children's books, among them *Thunderhoof* and *Three Fools and a Horse*, to spread out for kids on my old rug. But I forgot to ask Louise if I could set up in her yard. So I'll do Columbus Day in Brattleboro.

October 12: Off early Friday for Zora's last call in Vermont this year. When we arrived at the borrowed cabin I could smell the engine, hot, burned. The last four miles in was a steep climb.

I mix the boxes differently every time I set out so I'll encounter new titles as I rank them on my tables. Yesterday I bucked from the far corner of the barn some boxes I hadn't looked at since spring. Many of the books were damp and musty, their spines splotched with a sort of mold easily wiped off—but where did the wet come from? And how do sets get separated? Where is volume one of Rebecca West's *Black Lamb, Gray Falcon*? Where is volume one of *The History of Herodotus*? Why are some books I've bought marked "as is"? How could it be otherwise?

I made a fire in the cabin's box stove, then coffee—good smells. Jefe worked outside investigating holes and scents. But there were burrs. He came in a couple of times limping pitifully, his paws and undercoat prickling. At one point he stopped in a fringe of brush and started barking, wouldn't move. There was a thorn deep in one of his pads. As I pulled it out he licked my hand. I felt like Androcles. Outside in the cool air the smoke from our fire is a comfortable thing to smell. The fermenting leaves have an exotic fragrance, a blend of bourbon and dung.

A long row of black books on the cabin's bookshelves caught my eye: a complete *Arabian Nights*. It opens oddly,

"*And afterwards.*" I don't remember how long I read, because after flourishes to Allah the "*Story of King Shahryar and his Brother*" is about "*futtering*" as slaves and queens buss, wrap legs around "*as a button-loop clasps a button*," throw and enjoy each other for hours. Much about the faithlessness of women. The brothers are low on women as they themselves are taken by a Jinni's slave on threat of "*the illest of deaths*" if they won't "*do the deed of kind*" with the lady, "*white-skinned and of winsomest mien, of stature fine and thin, and bright as though a moon of the fourteenth night she had been, or the sun raining lively sheen.*" She commands them, "*Stroke me a strong stroke, without stay or delay.*" After some palaver they do.

There are footnotes ("*Debauched women prefer Negroes on account of the size of their parts. I measured one man in Somali-land who, when quiescent, numbered nearly six inches*"), rare words like "*quotha!*" and "*wotteth,*" which must be curdled King James or Richard Burton's approximation of Arab court speech, and overall a high heat that makes me wonder why this wonder isn't better known. The Burton Club edition was privately printed (no date). Only fear for my karma keeps me from lifting a volume or two.

When I went to rescue Jefe I noticed the apple trees. Two were bright with apples like Christmas balls. I shook the branches I could reach. From one tree, sixty small rose-coloreds, puckered and pocked, rust-streaked at the stem. They were crisp, slightly sweet. I parleyed with some cold-struck yellowjackets for the drops. I had a vision of applesauce.

I'm startled when someone hands me one of the books I've put out for sale and says, "You shouldn't sell this. You need to read it." Tom does that often. It's like making a gift. The

poet David Ray did it recently when he handed me Jung's
Memories, Dreams, Reflections.

I tried Jung while I boiled the applesauce. Maybe some
visions of futtering distracted me, but Jung was no go today.
His *"voice of being,"* as he puts it, didn't speak. I remind
myself that that's okay, I don't have to be up for every great
book all the time. I'm not yet ripe for Proust either, but I keep
those reputeds in reserve.

As the sun set Jefe and I walked over to North Pond, sniffed
around where we'd camped in May and I'd dunked in July.
No thought of swimming today. It's overcast and chilly, but
as we followed the curve of the pond around I noticed an
island off the far shore. We'll tie a boat to the van roof and
camp out there next year.

I poured some honey on my warm applesauce and it's fine.
Dark by 7:00. I'm surprised by the stillness, the cold, how
noisy the fire in the box stove is. It started raining. I put *Mother
Goose* beside my bed by way of homework but I didn't read
much when I lay down. Sweet it is to tuck in warm and dry, no
getting up or doing or leaving to think about for a while. Jefe is
deep in the sleeping bag with me making gruntled noises.
Mother Goose came to me in my drowse: *"Friday night's
dream / On the Saturday told, / Is sure to come true, / Be it
never so old."*

Saturday morning dawned clear and breezy. Reds, purples,
and yellows in the woods, a lot of sand-colored pine needles
showering down. Zora caught slowly with chattering noises
and a great spewing cloud of blue.

Given the rusted state of Zora's frame and the load aboard
I worried she might turn turtle going down the rocky wash-
board road I ground up yesterday. I kept her in first all the
way, pumping the brakes and my hand on the emergency. She

smoked but her knees held and we made it to my store-yard where the grass has spiked purple seed heads now. There are ragged pale-blue patches of a tiny flower.

No permit today. When Tom went to the town clerk she looked in her book and said, "Oh, you've had three. You only get three."

"*He's* had three," Tom said. "This one is for me."

"Nope, it's three for the place. Each place only gets three yard sales a year."

"This isn't a yard sale. We're selling books."

"'Personal property' is what it says. Books are personal property. Each place only gets to sell personal property three times a year."

"Stupid rule!" huffed Tom as he made for the door.

Set up anyway. Maybe we'll get shut down today, busted for selling books. I won't pack up on my own. I picture my confrontation with the state police, Brattleboro police, the Windham County sheriff. Handcuffs. Fines. Who enforces yard-sale permits?

It was early, 8:30, so cold my breath steamed. Not much traffic. Breakfast had been sketchy—tea, no coffee—so Jefe and I took off for a few minutes at Mocca Joe's. Bought a saucer of cream for my pal, a heavy mug of coffee for me, two scones for later, and charged my thermos.

I had the sign out by 9:00 in slanting yellow sunlight and started work on the tables. Traffic still thin. The woods are the color and feel of a bright nubby tweed. My hands are stiff with cold. Jefe's found a patch of warm sun on the passenger seat. I left the door open so he can keep an eye on things. Any passing dog is a big event.

My first caller was a garrulous retiree who lives across the street and wanted to tell me about researching his Gould family tree. A long blur of Goulds. He wasn't interested in books, he wanted to know what I'm doing. I offered him a Zora pamphlet but he wouldn't buy.

Then a bit of commerce for cheer and to cover the cost of getting here: a pair of stout freelance anthropologists who couldn't say what they were anthropologizing or for whom—"just general anthropology." I sold them the $6 book I was looking over when they arrived: William Cowper's letters, lately retired from the Philips Exeter Academy Library. They took it when I showed them this:

> *Olney, Nov. 9, 1784*
> *My Dearest Cousin,—Whose last most affectionate letter has run in my head ever since I received it, and which I now sit down to answer two days sooner than the post will serve me; I thank you for it, and with a warmth for which I am sure you will give me credit, though I do not spend many words in describing it. I do not seek new friends, not being altogether sure that I should find them, but have unspeakable pleasure in being still beloved by an old one. I hope that now our correspondence has suffered its last interruption, and that we shall go down together to the grave, chatting and chirping as merrily as such a scene of things will permit. . . .*
> *As for me, I am a very smart youth of my years: I am not indeed grown grey so much as I am grown bald. No matter. There was more hair in the world than ever had the honour to belong to me. . . .*
> *PS: That the view I give you of myself may be complete, I add the two following items—That I am in debt to nobody, and that I grow fat.*

I set up five tables and laid out an old Bokara rug with a scattering of children's books, the best among them Chaucer's *Chanticleer and the Fox*, its red cover faded and water-swelled, but the type is clear and its pictures make me smile. The rug's colors look wonderful on the fresh waxy grass, the last spurt of new green before the snow hits. I'm displaying about eight hundred books today, everything I own.

It was quiet for a while. I did some repricing as I set more books out, marking down some unwise purchases—boxed Literary Guild titles seem to put people off—sorting out duplicates. I have two *Admiral of the Ocean Sea*, two of Christopher Morley's *Parnassus on Wheels*—one of the happiest things to read. I'm looking in my boxes for Willa Cather titles, much asked for. Seem to be out of Laurie Lee.

Pinocchio caught me again, but before I could get full into how scared I used to be hearing that boy's terrifying dream, a worn blue Toyota arrived carrying an older woman, slight and quick with a friendly smile, and a girl, slower, tall, lumpy, her face closed. The mother started piling up books. The girl idled and visited with Jefe. She's about twelve. I pointed her to the rug. It looked inviting in the sun. Jefe joined her and lay down there.

I asked the woman what she collected.

"I don't collect, I sell. I do what you do, in Hanover— Dartmouth students and summer program people. Would you believe it? I'm the only street vendor selling used books."

As she ranged over my tables, cheerful and enthusiastic about title after title, she told me about her struggles with rigs, shelves, permits, insurance, what she sells, what she pays for books, what she likes to read. "Today it's Daudet's *Letters from My Windmill*."

I didn't know it. She promised to send me a copy. "I sell classics, Penguins, Oxfords, course books, thrillers, cookbooks. I get more for my books than you do, probably make more. I usually pay fifty cents for a good paperback, a dollar for hardbacks.

"You're expensive," she laughed, "but I'll sell what I buy here, just won't make as much as I like."

Her name is Carol. She took off her hat. Her hair is short, a graying sandy-blond, clear blue eyes, small, guarded for all her brisk friendliness. She told me she's a widow. Didn't say for how long or what happened to her husband or what she did before she got into bookselling. She's serious about her business, lists her inventory on computer, bought a software program with current book prices, another that helps her figure her taxes. She said she has seven thousand books in her basement and wants a space to show them all.

"People in town are getting to know me," she said. "I'd like a regular place they could come to. I have to go through an hour of setting up every day just to open. The weather can close me down fast when a storm comes. It closes me down absolutely mid-October to mid-April. And I can only show a little of what I have. I want a *real* bookshop! Got to do something soon because my car is giving out."

I mentioned my great-aunt Zora's style-shop, how she'd regarded keeping a store as giving a party.

"Exactly!" said Carol. "My customers are my friends. My work is my social life." She asked me why I got into this business.

"You come to a place as a stranger and the people you'd like to meet aren't looking around like kids willing to risk a new encounter. But they'll go out of their way to look at books. This is my way of making friends, staying alive, hearing stories. The people I meet tell me stories. Someone remarked, 'We tell stories when we cannot tell the truth,' but I don't think it's that way at all. Our stories are our truths."

"Have you kept up with anyone you've met doing this?"

I told her about the booksellers from Newfane who cleaned me out one weekend. The following week I stopped by to see their shop and we've written and visited back and forth several times since, even given each other books. There's the guy who's studying to be a teacher in northern Vermont. He's come back a couple of times, sent me his poetry and the syllabus for the course he's teaching at the community college. The Central Vermont Railroad man. A couple of others. A writer who lives around here.

She nodded as she browsed along. "I have a lot of repeat customers."

"Mine are mainly one-time encounters. There isn't time for much getting-to-know talk, but it's curious the willingness of people to tell you their stories if you ask them flat-out. Everybody has a story he wants to tell if he feels safe."

"Safe?" she asked.

"Not being thought silly or foolish for telling it. In a place for selling stories it's easy to get people to tell stories. It's like telling your life to a stranger on a bus as you travel through the night together, anything goes. You'll not be held to account."

"We tell stories to escape loneliness," Carol said without looking up.

Her daughter had passed over *Chanticleer* as too young for her so I told her the story, how they sang together, Chanticleer and the fair Demoiselle Partlet, *"polite, discreet, debonair, and companionable."* I told her how the fox caught Chanticleer in his pride and of Chanticleer's escape on a trick of praise. Got onto the moral in it, the truth of life about how we all like to be told how fine we are, how much we'll forgive or ignore about those who praise us.

I asked the girl what she remembered of *Pinocchio*. Only that his nose had grown with lying.

"I started reading it again this morning. It's not a fable or a wild tale. It's about how we live with one another."

A big puffing woman, shapeless in a quilted coat, walked over with a grocery bag of books to sell: a dozen Peter Pauper Press titles and a blue Oxford Classic copy of the book my

Rhode Island friend had mentioned, George Borrow's *The Bible in Spain*. This copy was logged in to the Coast Guard Academy Library on May 3, 1939, so it's almost exactly my age. Its once fine square shape is rounded from use so the covers don't quite lie trim, its pages smudged from thumbing but still in working order. Its condition and mine are about the same.

She explained that she was clearing her father's house, going around to flea markets offering his stuff to dealers. "Dust!" she exclaimed, dragging heavily on a little device she carries for asthma. She pointed to the back of her car awash with decorated cookie tins, a pair of alabaster lamps, bags of books tipped and spilling. She'd selected this particular bag for me. It felt lucky. She asked $9 and I gave it to her without a quibble. She was in a rush, didn't offer me any of the other bags.

Carol had gathered five boxes of history, travel, Penguin editions, biography, no fiction. She took *Pinocchio* and Sally Carrighar's *One Day at Teton Marsh* on my recommendation. I promised money back for any that didn't pour. When I made her daughter a present of *Chanticleer*, she came alive with a smile.

I'm getting good at adding in my head. Carol's total came to $168. She didn't question it. I took her check. Never dreamed I'd sell so much today. I'm getting over feeling badly about selling to dealers. We understand each other.

I was at the far table when I noticed a couple at the first one—a slight, short man in jeans and boots, maybe thirty, dark, and beside him a slender taller woman, very fair, younger, her hair cut in bangs, flowing tan slacks. I called hello and they waved. I thought he looked like a motorcycle type, but a few minutes later when I walked over to say hello I noticed how elegant he was: dark curled hair with some gray in it, oiled and pulled back, tied at the neck, pressed denims, fine tooled boots, a good tailored shirt open on his lean chest. For all his slimness, he's older than I thought, mid-forties. Brown eyes. We introduce. Pablo and Ann.

He'd picked up Richard Ellmann's *Oscar Wilde* and a Herman Hesse title. They were admiring a fine small edition of *Leaves of Grass* as I approached, laughing a little in their pleasure at finding it. They've just moved here, rented a house for two years, bookcases but few books. They were on their way to breakfast. "It's the one meal we go out for," said Ann, "when we saw your sign and stopped."

"What do you do?" I asked Pablo.

"I paint. I teach. In Montpelier."

"And you?" turning to Ann.

"I take care of Pablo."

"Lucky man."

"Yes," he said shyly, "I hope it lasts."

In a voice and manner as elegant as his body, but with a surprising intensity, he told me he's a student of Foucault. He escaped from Chile when his namesake Neruda did, and for the same reasons. He's interested in ecstatic ways of knowing.

"Perhaps there is no objective reality. Perhaps each of us— even the scientist, the mathematician—makes his own reality. Any work of history is at heart biography, the events shaped by the person writing it. As for ecstatic ways of knowing, well here's Whitman and Hesse," he said laughing.

They talked about ways of experiencing things, how the forest loses some of its magic and becomes an abstraction when you learn the names of the trees. I'd like to get to know these people, took their number.

11:30: Business was quiet and I was getting cold. Where's Tom? I moved into the van, crowding Jefe out of his sunny spot. He was willing to settle for a lap. Opened a bottle of my applesauce, the thermos, broke out the scones. Jefe found the scone agreeable. I leafed through *The Bible in Spain*. It will prove a hard book to finish.

I rooted around for something livelier, hit on Frank Morley's *The Great North Road*, found it wonderful for the "Farewell" that opens it. Morley returned to London after World War II to find the city he loved and all his haunts and runs in ruins. But:

> *I had heard that when all the buildings hereabouts were razed to their cellars, there had been disclosed a long, continuous section of the northern face of the original Roman Wall of London. Concealed for the many centuries, the north front of the Wall was now disclosed in length and to its full height, as it was* ab urbe condita. *As had many people, I had seen bits and pieces of the Wall before. . . . Now one had a continuity in all its courses, from the original Roman stonework foundations to the medieval brickwork at the top. Along the whole northern face of the Wall holes had been pecked into it as the housings of a thousand years and more had attempted to jostle each other and to nestle against it. If your mind's eye could get down to the ground level—the ground level as it had been in Boadicea's time— you could see the Wall standing as a cliff, as a rock cliff facing the north with a fierce, angry hardness.*

My hair rises at the telling of such stuff, and what a teller Morley is! As he walked north through the rubble, taking his bearing from the "riding redoubtable dome of Paul," he found himself on the line of the Great North Road. He thought about England's history in its traffic of nearly two thousand years: *"Caesar and the Roman Empire and the Roman Church; Cromwell and the British Empire and the English Bible"*— four hundred miles, London to Edinburgh. *"The Great North Road had carried—well, now, what hadn't it carried, and how far, and where not, around the world?"* And so this book. I kept it and paid myself for the day.

At last another caller, a very dressed-up woman. Her husband drove their Town Car up close to where I was standing and left the motor running. She got out slowly, carefully, keeping things in place. She was important. They were on their way to something important. "I am specifically looking for Readers Digest Condensed Books. I have a series I am trying to complete," she said very sternly.

She had already turned away and was toiling back into the Lincoln before I thought to ask what the series was.

Tom arrived at noon, a little tender on his feet it seemed, but cheery. He brought a big pot of yellow chrysanthemums to grace the table nearest the road and a lunch basket from Mary— apples (staples here in picking time), buttermilk, and two big wedges of squash pie. She's not going to make it here today. She and a neighbor are getting ready for a tag sale on Terrace Street, Brattleboro's best address. Their offerings ought to be pretty good. Mary's mother died last year. They've been clearing out a lot of china, pottery, small furniture, and cooking gear. No books. Tom won't sell any but he gives away a lot. And no clothing. Mary wears everything she gets to ribbons. Frayed and faded, things assume a certain elegance on her gaunt frame.

He quickly circled the tables. "You really shouldn't sell this if you haven't read it," he said handing me *The Yellow Wallpaper*, a slight thing, barely thirty pages. "You'll never forget it. And this," he added, "you must keep this, too. An inspired book. I've read it two or three times." It was Josephine Tey's *The Daughter of Time*.

Then he picked up a Zola title. That got us talking about Cézanne, Tom maintaining that Zola was the best friend Cézanne ever had. I told him how hurt Cézanne was when his old chum came to Aix and ignored him. Cézanne was on his way to Zola's hotel when someone told him that when asked whether he was going to see his friend, Zola had answered, "Why should I bother with that dead one?"

Over lunch I noticed a tallish woman, my age. I caught her eye and waved. She smiled. She had a big head, fleshy face, dark eyes, and long flowing dyed black curls that made her look like an aging Cavalier. She opened a book and sniffed it. I was tickled to see her do that, the mark of a true bibliophile. Tom got started on Proust and smells and quoted Kipling: *"Smells are surer than sounds or sights to make the heart strings crack."* A younger man had joined her. She bought him our offerings of Faulkner and Stendhal.

I told her what I remembered of Faulkner's Nobel Prize address: *"I decline to accept the end of man. It is easy enough to say that man is immortal simply because he will endure: that when the last ding-dong of doom has clanged and faded from the last worthless rock hanging tideless in the last red and dying evening, that even then there will still be one last sound: that of his puny inexhaustible voice, still talking. I refuse to accept this. I believe that man will not merely endure: he will prevail. He is immortal, not because he alone among creatures has an inexhaustible voice, but because he has a soul, a spirit capable of compassion and sacrifice and endurance."*

"Wow!" she said.

"About the time Faulkner got the Nobel Prize Senator Joe McCarthy was screaming about Reds in Washington. In school they were teaching us to 'duck and cover' against the inevitable atomic blast. 'The last ding-dong of doom' didn't seem far-off. Faulkner gave us hope."

She nodded. "We all thought we were going to get it. I wonder if any other generation was so sure of its annihilation. *On the Beach* and stuff like that. That's why we're such hedonists. It's something I'm writing about."

She says she supports herself writing. Must be one of the few.

I showed her Kawabata's *Snow Country* and *Thousand Cranes*. "Another Nobel winner. Beautiful stories. He called his Nobel address, 'Japan the Beautiful and Myself,' wrote about being a man of feeling in traditions of Buddhism, Oriental painting, flower arranging, the tea ceremony—things that figure in his writing."

Before I could get our writer's name a sturdy woman joined us, energy in her walk, energy in her kinky hair. She looks strong. A smoker. Said she was looking for books on the labor movement for a friend in Ohio and did we know how good things are in Ohio? A lot of jobs in Ohio. She's from Maine, no jobs in Maine, no justice there either. A judge is doing her out of her interest in an estate. We talked about what's become of the labor movement. Her daughter appeared, that same hair only gold like wire and she was tanned and round, beautiful in a full way. She's a student at Marlboro College up the road. Tom found the mother Thorstein Veblen's *Theory of the Leisure Class* and she turned up something on the cane cutters in Puerto Rico. The lovely girl found *Emma*. Her lips are very red.

Our bag woman from the summer struggled by slowly but did not turn in when we waved. She looks thinner. As she shambled along bent over her bulging bags she seemed to be dragging one foot. In the sunlight her hair blazed.

The man who'd stopped on Memorial Day looking for physics and went off with a book about crabs showed up today for Robert Burns. His name is Henry. He's a weather-beaten Yankee with a lot of gray-white hair and small, black measuring eyes sunk deep in his head. He wore an old Army trenchcoat with a blanket buttoned-in and faded campaign patches. He told us what a sweet-voiced lover Burns was, how women had swooned to his singing "*Jamie, come try me*," and the many consequences of his *hough-magandie*, not least his day standing in Kirk for adultery. Henry said he wanted a book with the songs, he had a good voice still. The *New Oxford Book of English Verse* does Burns no justice with its prim selections. We came up with a *Selected Letters* but Henry wouldn't part with his money for that. "It's the songs I want, the poetry he sang 'em." He told us that the songs Burns is best known for, like *Auld Lang Syne*, he didn't write but copied down from an old man.

On a whim I told Henry a line that had stuck in my head— *"Like Lewis & Clark we come with what we need, nothing more, / Consume ourselves voyaging"*—and showed him the *Journal*s of Lewis & Clark. I told him about their care in packing and stashing, especially the powder they needed which was sealed in lead bags they could melt for the right amount of shot, the sufficiency of it all. He took it.

We directed him to the town library for Burns and perhaps a taste of Burton's *Arabian Nights*. Turns out Tom has a complete Burton plus six volumes of "Supplemental Nights," which defy my imagining. "When you hit the *Nights* pay attention to the tale of Barmecide," Tom advised. "It'll help you plan your concerts."

A stocky, rolling, black-haired woman had quietly joined our party. She was reserved at first, but Tom drew her out when he asked if she knew any Robert Burns bawdy. She's about my shape, mid-fifties with hazel eyes and a long, slow chuckle. Her skin is soft and milk-colored with tiny lines around her eyes and mouth. She speaks slowly with an elegant old grandmother's exactness. She told us her name is Alice and she's an independent scholar, a social scientist, doesn't know much about Burns. She has a part-time job right now taping and editing narratives of New York civil service workers, getting them to talk about how they feel about their work.

I put her onto something I'd just discovered: Robert Schrank's *Ten Thousand Working Days*—a master machinist in the 1930s and '40s writing about union organizing and how important schmoozing and playfulness are in the workplace, how important pride in craftsmanship is.

Henry and Tom talked about factory work. Tom was on a Chrysler line in Detroit for a while after the war, said he was closer to his buddies there than any he ever met teaching. Only actors and musicians seem to have as much fun together.

Alice asked if there is pride of craftsmanship in office work. I told them about the old lawyers I worked with at Edwards and Angell in Providence when I was starting out. They had the grinning pleasure kids have when they get something difficult exactly right, the pride of craftsmen about the wills and trusts and deeds they drafted, pride in how their clients trusted them. I never met with quite the same again in the other law offices where I worked—but they'd pretty much shuffled all the old lawyers out to make way for the young money-makers.

Alice told us she makes most of what she lives on by taking groups of American artists on USIA-sponsored cultural exchange trips abroad. She's a good linguist, goes out for two or three months a year, has the rest of her time open for writing. On her last assignment she guided Bela Fleck and the Flecktones to Ulan Baatar. The Flecktones are a three-man string band from Nashville. Bela is a white man in his early thirties; his partners are black, one named Victor who plays bass, the other a percussionist named "Futureman" who plays the drumitar, his own invention. By her account they and their twenty-six trunks plus ladies made quite a hit in Mongolia.

The cold was wearing. Alice left for a cup of something warming at Mocca Joe's and a shot at the *Times* crossword. She bought the Schrank and offered me the books in a Greenwich Village apartment a friend had just vacated, mainly feminist titles, some children's, all free for the taking. Rain promised for tomorrow so I said I'd drive down.

A customer came back complaining that I'd oversold Victor Hugo to him a few weeks ago. He was strangely mollified when I read aloud from Roger Shattuck's *The Banquet Years* a description of the state funeral the French put on when Hugo died.

"They were glad it was over," my complainer growled. He'd bought the complete.

Another man walked up fast, all business, no cordials. "A dictionary? Gotta have a dictionary."

We had an exhausted Webster's "Collegiate" in frail covers for a dollar.

"Perfect," he said.

"What are you looking up?" Tom wanted to know.

"Nothing. I'm a cartoonist. Need it for a picture."

Two boys, age nine or ten, had been idling around. Suddenly the tall one seized a big volume. They scuffled over it, the stocky dark one yelling, "But you don't have any money."

"Yes I do," from the other.

"How much is this book?"

"Two dollars."

The tall kid produced the money. The book looked like a novel. *Lizzie*.

They headed up the hill. I began to worry. What had I sold them? It was a book I'd gotten from one of the barn boxes. Was this something boys should read? I yelled for them to come back.

"May I look at the book you bought?"

As the tall one handed it to me he said, "My dad and I are going to spend a night in the house where it happened."

"I'm gonna go, too, maybe," piped the stocky one.

Lizzie: Lizzie Borden. The ax and forty whacks lady.

"Okay, thanks." I handed it back to him. What do you say to family-sponsored mayhem? It's like watching violent TV together.

Trade grew fitful, then downright desultory. There's a yard sale on across the street—lamps, woks, a Belgian waffle maker, file cabinets, an old backpack. They outdraw us ten to one with a lot of pickup trucks. Pickups don't stop for us but bicyclers do. I sold a book on building a cathedral to a biker. He slipped it into his backpack and resumed his peddle to Bennington *ex cathedra*.

Tom's always been a fancy dresser for all he's had no money. I asked him about it in the lull. Turns out that when he left high school he went to work in a men's store, learned about mohair and mogadore, barathea and challis, broadcloth and pima cotton, learned to buy the best, new and used. So even in threadbares there's a hint of the dandy about him.

He picked up *The Canterbury Tales* and got lost in it for a while. Then he gave me this, a drunken tough accosting an old man:

> *Why live so long? Isn't it time to die?*
> *The old, old fellow looked him in the eye*
> *And said, 'Because I never yet have found,*
> *Though I have walked to India, searching round*
> *Village and city on my pilgrimage,*
> *One who would change his youth to have my age.*
> *And so my age is mine and must be still*
> *Upon me, for such time as God may will.*
> *Not even Death, alas, will take my life;*
> *So, like a wretched prisoner at strife*
> *Within himself, I walk alone and wait*
> *About the earth, which is my mother's gate . . .'*

On to Jonathan Swift and why he was so tormented. We had Swift on our tables. Tom remembered Swift's epitaph,

"*Jonathan Swift lies here where furious indignation can no longer wring his heart.*"

I asked Tom what he wants for his epitaph. He shook his head slowly. "I don't believe there is any hereafter, I think this is it."

"Yes, but for an epitaph—for those remaining after you're gone, how would you legend yourself for their remembering?"

He smiled. "I like Keats's, '*Here lies one whose name was writ in water.*' He didn't make it up, he heard it somewhere. And dead at twenty-eight. Jesus!"

Then he gave us from memory this by Callimachus as some of the most moving lines of remembering and regret he ever came upon:

> *They told me, Heraclitus, they told me you were dead,*
> *They brought me bitter news to hear and bitter tears*
> > *to shed.*
> *I wept as I remembered how often you and I*
> *Had tired the sun with talking and sent him down*
> > *the sky.*
>
> *And now that thou art lying, my dear old Carian guest,*
> *A handfull of gray ashes, long, long ago at rest,*
> *Still are thy pleasant voices, thy nightengales, awake;*
> *For Death, he taketh all away, but them he cannot take.*

For a change of mood we rummaged together in Swift's *Journal for Stella.*

For February 5, 1711: "*Morning . . . I wish my cold hand was in the warmest place about you, young women. I'd give ten guineas upon that account with all my heart, faith; oh, it starves my thing; so I'll rise and bid you good morrow, my ladies both, good morrow. Come stand away, let me rise! Patrick, take away the candle. Is there a good fire?—So—up a-dazy.*"

That sold our Swift. The Chaucer went, too. But Tom wasn't really trying to sell them, he wanted people to love them, to feel for them what he did—as if a book is not so much an object of commerce as a spurt of life, a thing of passion.

I found something for Tom in the 1940 *New Directions* anthology, Wright Morris's "Peter Finley": *"My cane has the carved head of a dog, smooth hollow sockets are his eyes. Walking I keep my fingers there. I can feel him check me at a rise and lead where objects fall away. Space is a thing we lean upon. We can feel my son's new love affair as he stoops and tips my head to shave. My wife's patience rises from her hair. We can read a storm and hear a color glow—in the sun we can smell a sparrow's fear. But to die is a thing we do not know. Yet of an evening it whispers, rocks our chair."*

"Yes," he said after a moment, "that has the magic. It lifts you out and leaves goosebumps."

A skinny, blond, surprisingly hairy young man came by in a well-kept old VW he's obviously very proud of. He looks to be in his late twenties, a wedge-shaped face, slender hands, long fingers, his clothes droopy—an Appalachian type. He scouted and scouted and finally found one thing, a 75¢ *Where Angels Fear to Tread*.

"I've heard of it. Is it good?" he wanted to know. I sketched the story.

He pondered and looked some more. I asked his name, where he came from. He was a social worker in Philly for nine years, taught adult education courses for people on welfare—basic math and writing skills to help them get jobs. He said most of his students didn't want to be on welfare. They took their classes seriously and a good percentage went on to work.

"But now they want them up and out," Rick said. "No time for my ten-week courses. The federal funds for that have been cut."

It sounded like Henry VIII closing down the monasteries. Students and their teachers cast out again in pursuit of some new theology, this time balanced budgets.

Rick is looking for work. He put his book back. "Guess I have enough books for right now," he said. He had no place to stay, had to get on to find a campsite. Tom made him a present of the book.

"By the time they get the budget balanced and the deficit paid off we'll all be out of work," I told Tom.

Sunday morning I drove down to New York to collect the books Alice had offered. The place is just off Washington Square where the sidewalks are thick with book dealers' tables. I'm going to join them soon. I asked a bearded young dealer in Jung and incense if I'd need a permit.

"No man, just a tax number man, you gotta collect the tax for Albany, man."

Thirty-two cartons from Alice's friend. Up four narrow twisting steep flights of stairs, then down with loads that barely cleared the walls. Two hundred and fifty-six flights in all. I felt those stairs the next day and the day after. Didn't need to jog.

I found some good things, among them the *Langston Hughes Reader* published by Braziller in 1958, and this banging title, *All the Women Are White, All the Blacks Are Men, But Some of Us Are Brave*. There were two waddling cats in the apartment. The books were steeped in cat. Jefe sniffed the boxes with some curiosity when I got home.

While I was hauling those boxes down the endless stairs a runny-nosed old guy held the door for me at one point. "You movin' in? Don't. They keep it too cold."

When I told him what I was about he smiled and invited me in. Introduced himself as Murray, says he used to be a book dealer.

He lives in two small rooms, piles of books and notebooks around, a broken table, stuff layered and grimy like he'd survived a shipwreck a long time ago. Fresh newspapers were spread on the floor. There were the stumps of two backless chairs. He sat on one very straight. His slenderness makes him look tall. He has a handsome narrow head like a sculpture of an old Roman, dark teeth with a lot of gold, thick dark gray hair worn long and combed back. At eighty-five his profile is beaked, crow-like, grooved, the color of an old Indian. His eyes are large, black, clear, in-taking. He wore a finely made purple sweater with bone buttons at the throat. His smile is almost feminine, his voice sweet, gentle, a singer's voice.

Murray talked about going on buying trips into western Pennsylvania, collecting thirty to fifty cartons of books at a time: "I had a good time running around—the happiest days of my life—alone in the truck. Needed little to live on in those days, a dollar for a bed, a dollar for a good meal. Free to come and go. If I had a hunch I'd go to a place. There were big houses then, estates, people collected books, made libraries." He gave me as his best advice: "In the used book business, it isn't what you sell 'em for; it's what you buy 'em for."

I asked how he got into the book business, what he got out of it.

"I grew up in the thing. Gave up college life at the end of one term. 'A's in languages, failed everything else. My father founded Dauber & Pine in the mid-1920s at 66 Fifth Avenue, a big operation for that kind of trade, maybe fifty thousand titles. We sold anything, new and used.

"As for what I got out of it? A lot of good hard labor and book dust. Old bookmen seem to get a good longevity out of it. I've swallowed tons and tons of old book dust. That and the lifting up and putting down of book boxes is the best thing you get out of the trade. No time to read."

He wouldn't talk about his politics but it came out that he'd joined the Lincoln Brigade, gone to Spain in '37, got sick and was shipped home. He was twenty-eight at the time.

"Why did you go?"

"It was a chance to get a crack at Adolph. Your neighbor's house is on fire, you don't wait until yours catches fire before you go to help put it out. I saw what Hitler was doing, his plan. There was a wonderful Miró poster that said it all, but I've lost it."

I asked about his favorite titles. He looked off for a moment. "Arnold Bennett's *Journals*. I like journals, books of letters, stuff creative people write. You can see how he used his journals in *Old Wives Tale*—a great book."

"What are you reading now?" I asked.

"A lot of things, an old geology text I picked up, Pavese in the Italian. I'm studying Italian as I go along."

"Have you written about your life?"

"No writing. A terrible resistance to letters and writing!"

He mentioned one of his friends, Seymour Hacker, an art-book dealer. "He joined the Merchant Marine before World War II. He'd stock up on cigarettes, take 'em to Europe, trade 'em for art books, books on the decorative arts. Built up quite a business that way. Then it was the 1960s and civil rights. Seymour ran two bookmobiles down into the South, went to the black campuses selling books, into the small black towns, built a good trade with those bookmobiles."

I took my leave when he apologized for going on so long. He acted as if I'd done him an honor by coming in.

I like Seymour Hacker's idea. Maybe I'll try some of the smaller Southern college towns next year—places where they're hungry enough to appreciate my $1.25 Penguins and $3 World Classics, not too proud to add a $4 Harvard Classic Chaucer or *Piers Plowman* or Samuel Johnson to their shelves. But first to a rich town, Charlottesville, Jefferson's place.

CHAPTER 14

To Charlottesville

November 8: The frost this morning reveals the ground's lines and wrinkles. It will burn off by 10:00, but I'm ready to head south to the warm.

I was snugged in my book room, resolved to get a start on figuring my taxes before I headed off when Claude, my ever-welcome UPS man, arrived with Elvis on his tapedeck and a box of surprises for me. I'd worked out a trade with a book-dealing friend in the Catskills, sent her stuff from our basement—old horsebells, a Victorian eggbeater, some battered, silver-plated child's cups, and an assortment of green glass bottles. She in turn sent me junkers from her shelves, among them forty essays by Guy Davenport, *The Geography of the Imagination*. Surefire for Charlottesville.

North Point Press of San Francisco published the essays on good paper in bound signatures with a paper cover in 1981, before their real-estate angel ran dry. They must have known they'd lose money on this. It's the kind of book that's fun to press on the maybe-willing. Davenport's is a vivid, kinky style that erupts now and then in lines that end up snagged in memory: "*Geography is the wife of history, as space is the wife of time.*" That's out of the jumbled show-and-tell title essay about white foxes, okra, Poe, Spengler, China, Sears Roebuck, calico, and interior decorating.

I once had Davenport as a teacher. He lectured on Pound, Stein, and Joyce, opened the class by drawing a large Chinese ideogram to explain the evolution of language. Letters started out as pictures and got abstracted down to the black-and-white marks of our alphabet to make stories, evoke desire, memory, tears, fury, joy, longing. Those patterns of strange marks we read work more magic than the dots that trace the way to water. Davenport's book is that lecture. Everything is signature.

A copy of St. Augustine's *Confessions,* with a revealing note that his master, Ambrose, was one of the first to read without moving his lips, also rolled down from the Catskills. (Imagine the murmurings in the scriptorium—so many insects in a wheat field on a hot afternoon.) And in a biography of Tennyson, " *'Violets, man, violets! Smell them and you'll sleep better,' he exclaimed, falling to his knees.*"

There was a broken copy of Lin Yutang's *The Importance of Living,* published in 1937, a title I'd not ordinarily be drawn to save that my father had one. He didn't keep much. He was a spare man. Yutang holds that human happiness is sensuous. In the examples he gives I hear my father. He quotes Thoreau on the creak of crickets, Whitman on the scent and murmur of falling snow, someone else on distinguishing between the odors of noon and midnight, or of winter and summer, or of a windy spell and a still one. Yutang gives a seventeenth-century Chinese aristocrat's "thirty-three happy moments," which he counted with a friend one day when rainy weather kept them in. One: *"To cut with a sharp knife a bright green watermelon on a big scarlet plate of a summer afternoon. Ah, is this not happiness?"*

I loaded Zora with a dozen boxes, maybe 250 of my best titles (in the process scrapping a lot of the special-interest, crime, politics, and fiction I'd picked up in New York a few weeks before). I left a good broad sleeping space stuffed with a camp mattress, fitted Jefe with a fresh box and a retired feather quilt tucked in a sleeping bag, water, a pint of dark Jamaican rum, tins of canned milk and sardines, a thermos of coffee, some oranges and new apples, and Alpo and dog cookies. For equipment, a thermometer, my Gaz burner, and a portable CD player with headphones. Off at 4:00 A.M. for the Blue Ridge.

Jefe remembered our previous trips and sang out for all his old stops. In Philadelphia, we stopped by George Allen's to see if he had any free boxes. Nothing free this time, but on the cheap shelf he keeps outside a copy of *Lolita*, the International Collectors Library's faux leather edition, good, clear type on fine-ribbed cream paper—a very nice job with gold embossing on the cover and a ribbon place marker sewn in, plus an afterword by the author. No exact scent to give away the whereabouts of its past, no indication that this *Lolita* was ever possessed save for what looks like a dog bite on the back cover. At the start: *"Lolita, light of my life, fire of my loins, my sin, my soul. Lo-lee-ta: the tip of the tongue taking a trip of three steps down the palate to trip, at three, on the teeth. Lo. Lee. Ta."* Hard to put down.

I also picked up a *Madame Bovary*, about which Flaubert, dying, raged that *he* would die while Emma, that whore of his creation, would live. Indeed, in my hands.

For 45¢ more Vita Sackville-West's *A Joy of Gardening* in paperback, much worn. This book has been read; it has a good, strong, musty smell, whiskey and wood fires in its past, a pretty cover of large, looping poesy rings, some entries marked by a prior owner, including *"The Christmas rose,* Helleborus niger, *in high Dutch called Christ's herb, 'because it flowereth about the birth of our Lord.' . . . The Christmas rose has been for centuries in our gardens. Spenser refers to it in the* Faerie Queene, *and it is described as early as 1597 in his* Herball *by John Gerard, who considered that a purgation of hellebore was 'good for mad and furious men.' "*

Surely folks in Charlottesville will delight in these and allow me to multiply the $2.25 I laid out for them. As I got ready to pay, George looked up and said in his usual deep way, "Will you wear them out or would you like a bag?"

We wobbled south through Maryland with regular infusions of motor oil and stops for my companion owing to the fragrant novelties of exotic flora and fauna (not to mention Roy Rogers' chicken, which Jefe will tell you goes down kinda' easy). We passed signs bearing the state's flag brave with Lord Baltimore's flashy black and orange and a good mix of names, Indian ones like Wicomico and Chesapeake and some grand old English ones like Howard, Cecil, and Calvert.

As we went along I thought about how buying books almost at retail is draining me pretty fast. I've started to advertise to buy libraries: "Good used books wanted, hardcover and paperback, biography, history, autobiography, journals, letters, classics, essays, belle lettres, poetry. We have a truck and a vacuum cleaner, so we'll take everything and clean up after. Please write describing what you have."

My ads have run for a month. So far I've been offered one library, had five calls about old bibles, and heard from two people possessed of inscribed garden books.

I passed up going to see the garden books. My one invitation to clear out and clean up a whole library was from a retiring pastor. Little did I expect to find in gleaming first editions the steaming, lubricious bare-my-everything fictions and tell-alls of the last twenty-five years. His shelves groaned like a mouth with too many teeth, books stuffed, grooved, and piled on the floor, the case-tellers and storytellers outnumbering the theologians and philosophers one hundred to one. I had to let it go, but I'd take in one of his sermons anytime.

I bought two of the King James Bibles I was offered, well-made things on India paper. If every book were so well-made, libraries would last forever; and if every book were so well-written? People don't seem to buy them to read; they sell like dictionaries and cookbooks: People who need to look something up come over and ask, "Do you have _____?" I've never sold one to a browser but a browser recently showed me "a text for a sermon to booksellers" in John: *"And there are also many other things which Jesus did, the which, if they should be written every one, I suppose that even the world itself could not contain the books that should be written."*

When David Ray was moving he sent me four boxes from his library. I paid what I could, but any sum would have been insultingly small. *"Pricing a book is one of the most poignant forms of criticism,"* Anatole Broyard confides in *Kafka Was the Rage*, his brief memoir of Greenwich Village right after World War II when he opened a bookshop and advertised for stock. Sadly, he liked books but he didn't like the people his books attracted:

> *What I hadn't realized was that, for many people, a bookshop is a place of last resort, a kind of moral flophouse. Many of my customers were the kind of people who go into a bookshop when all other diversions have failed them. Those who had no friends, no pleasures, no resources came to me. . . .*
>
> *It was the talkers who gave me the most trouble. Like the people who had sold me books, the talkers wanted to sell me their lives, their fictions about themselves, their philosophies. . . . As they talked on, I thought of all the junk I had carried out of the shop—the boilers, bathtubs and radiators. These people were bringing it all back.*

Going over Ray's books I thought about how a reader reveals himself in small ways: how he signs them, tags that indicate where the book was purchased, notes, underlinings, things tucked in over the years. Inscriptions, notes, and underlinings are the most revealing. I usually curse the underliners and won't buy their books, but once, by luck, I ended up with John Lehman's copy of William Plomer's *Autobiography*. Lehman's tiny, tidy, pencil notes in the margin tell of his occasional skepticism and frequent enthusiasm. Opposite Plomer's *"Not at all an ancestor-worshipper, I can't resist a character,"* Lehman wrote, "Glorious! The odd, the freakish, the eccentric—love of odd stories, the odder the more it was treasured in his mind, the funnier he found it."

Jefe and I camped in the mountains an hour or so out of Charlottesville. We saw staring eyes and trees glowing phosphorescent in our lights. Jefe stayed very close to me, tense, his nose and ears alert to protect us. There were hawks, ravens, and turkey vultures in the dawn. It was cold as Canada at 3400 feet—thirty-five degrees, not much more than that inside the van. Our breath had fogged the windows in the night. The dog shivered miserably when I hauled him out of the sleeping bag for his necessaries, sulked with his stub tail down until restored to his nest. I warmed his food a little. For me, sardines and sweet hot chocolate laced with coffee—a sovereign wake-up for any chilled book dealer. I stripped and sponged and shaved in the side view mirror, very awake when I hit the mall.

A friend in Charlottesville had worked things out with the town bureaucrats so that I could set up Saturday morning: a lot of red tape and black crepe. I had to pay $32 for a "Certificate of Appropriateness" (Am I a felon? Have I molested anyone? Do I carry arms? Do I trade in contraband? Are my goods wholesome?) good for that weekend only. It was required that I drape my table (no more than ten-feet long and four-feet deep) with black cloth brushing the ground. We are becoming a nation of niggled permitees.

I started setting up at 8:00, propped a little "Zora" sign on a bench near my table. Had one row of books out when a hearty munching couple arrived, a trencherman and his buxom moll working their way through sticky buns from the bakery, the kind of buns that are thick and juicy with raisins and buttered cinnamon inside, round and golden. They'd only bought one each. A poor policy.

Right away they found things. That was cheering, for all they didn't share their treats. So I started showing them the good things I was pulling from my boxes: Marcia Davenport's *Too Strong for Fantasy*—sold—and then Iris Origo's wonderful autobiography, *Images and Shadows*, sold when I showed them this: *"Why then am I writing this book at all, and what sort of a book would I like it to be? Desmond MacCarthy once remarked, at Mr. Asquith's breakfast table, that there are only three motives for writing an autobiography: St. Augustine's, Casanova's or Rousseau's—'either because a man thinks he has found "The Way," or to tell what a splendid time he has had, and enjoy it again by describing it, or to show—well, that he was a much better fellow than the world supposed.' 'I'm glad to hear you say that,' said Mr. Asquith, who was cutting himself a slice of ham. 'That is just what I am trying to do.' "*

A blissed-out, gaping fat man passed by slowly and settled on a nearby bench. In response to my hello he said he'd noticed I had Allen Ginsberg's *Howl* and what was it about. When I quoted the lines I remembered, *"I see the best minds of my generation / starving, hysterical, naked,"* he observed, "Sounds like he got on some bad dope."

By 10:00 the air was saturated with the fine smell of coffee roasting, breezes from the surrounding rolling green mountains, boxwood whiffs, a few last roses, the sounds of the fountain and John the singer. John got Jefe barking on his first pass. He was tall, slim, black, with straightened hair slicked down, pressed jeans, not young. He strode past us, slow and elegant, the sun on him, his eyes straight ahead, singing loud and strong, "True love [pause, a few steps] is hard to find."

He walked by again, later, the same slow-paced, high-gaited saunter and looked over. I smiled and said I liked his singing. He came over and we introduced. He has a strong handshake, a test. I gave it my best and he smiled, that too slow-paced and measured, with a lot of gold.

"You've got a good handshake," he said.

"So do you."

He nodded. His eyes lock in, don't swerve. "Folks got to get along," he said. Then, "What you got on special today?"

I allowed as how all my books are special, but I held up Lin Yutang's *The Importance of Living* and pointed him to my favorite part, the "Thirty-Three Happy Moments."

"The Importance of Living," he said. "Women know about that. They know about that because they bring life into being. They suffer. Men don't suffer what women suffer. And they live longer. You tell me."

I told him I thought he was a singer and a preacher.

He looked over the book. "I do some preaching and I do some singing, but mainly I play bass."

He stood there motionless, unwrinkled, immaculate, spare, no loose gestures, everything about him measured out and a little bit amused as if he knows what a show he makes. "I think I'll take this book. I think this book is a sign. How much is this book?"

It was $4. He eased some bills out of his pants. He had $4, just.

"I don't want to clean you out."

"Clean me out? I got money in that bank right there. I'm on my way to that bank. I'll be okay about my money."

"Well, thank you," I said. "You've given me something this morning."

He smiled that slow opening-up smile. "You've given me something," and he put out his hand for another long, hard handshake. His skin is coppery black. Maybe he's part Indian, his pace and handshake part of an Indian rite.

"Would you give me another song?"

He sucked in his breath and leveled at me without pause or blinking, *"Nobody knows / The trouble I've seen,"* strong and rich like fine coffee and with such sudden force and intensity that the people standing around started back a little.

"Thank you, John."

"You're welcome," he said with a slow nod, and without more, he went off in his straight-line parade march way.

My near neighbor on the mall was a Black Muslim dealer in oils, essences, joss sticks, and pamphlets. Early on he asked me to spell him while he went off for coffee. He did the same for Jefe and me. I asked if anybody ever checked on his certificate.

"They come by for dope," he said. "The plainclothes. Never had anybody ask for my papers, but I hear they'll get you if you don't have the cloth."

By 11:00 we had Irish music. That brightened Jefe as it seemed to bring out more people with dogs.

While setting up I'd noticed two scruffy guys skulking around, one older, maybe forty, his face pocked, his clothes looking like he'd had a hard night. His companion was a tall boy not yet twenty, almost gaunt with a cleanly handsome if sallow face. He looked pretty rumpled too and wore strange, orange-lensed glasses. They circled around looking for a place to settle. A couple of very old, caved-in, cigarette-sucking locals shuffled over and joined them. They settled on a nearby bench and tuned up for the sweetest, most rollicking, dancing, lilting, frolicking, whirligig, toe-tapping round of reels and jigs and Irish tunes I've ever heard. Now and then one of the ancients would spell the boy on the guitar, but he was the best and it was just a smiling courtesy on his part to let the walking dead aboard. He had a winsome boy's smile when folks put money in his guitar case. They did Scots songs too, ballads, somber ones, gleeful ones, Italian songs, Spanish tunes, on and on. They played almost non-stop until 1:00.

A couple of times during the morning a handsome old man with eyes of a surprising cornflower-blue canvassed my table. He was drawn but wary, like some rare bird circling my feeder asking himself, "Is this a trap?" He'd look, leave, then idle back. Finally I caught his eye and said hello. He was formal, reserved. I took him for a professor. He's a foreign service officer named Blake, just back from a posting in Iceland, where there are more bookstores per capita than anywhere else in the world. He said he likes books, has a lot of books, but he's getting rid of books, he doesn't need any more books. He's at a point where he reads something then goes to a shelf for something else he has that relates to that, then remembers another book out on his front porch that has some bearing on the subject at hand, and soon he's barricaded in his chair. I can see why he doesn't need any more books.

I sympathized, but there he was, the moth drawn to my light, the fly to my sticky paper. And sure enough, on his fourth pass he went right to Boswell's *Tour of the Hebrides* and said he'd take it. He told me he has two other copies but my edition has Pottle's introduction and he had to have it, so there was another $7 in my pocket.

Another moth was a beautiful, big Luna—a student at the university, who moaned as she sidled by, "Oh! Why are you doin' this to me? I don't *need* any more books."

She picked up a Rabelais, the Modern Library Nietzsche, Prescott's two volume *Conquest of Peru*. Her bill came to $16. She handed me a $20 with little bleats of mourning, loss, guilt, and pleasure. Then she spotted something else, one of my pricier things, Melville's *Typee* in a slipcased edition. I gave her the lot for her $20 and asked if she still felt bad about stopping. "No," she laughed. "I got bargains. I'm ahead."

It was an easy friendly crowd. An ample older woman in a flowing silky robe walked by, laughing and talking with a well-turned-out man. She admired my table and picked up something. We introduced. "We're off to Atlanta," the man said. "We're the Olympic Gossip Team." He's a dean in the law school; she's a retired librarian. She said they were having coffee up the way when a friend came in and said, "You've got to go see the used-book dealer out there." She told me I'm the only book dealer she's ever seen on the mall and I beat hollow the prices of the used-book stores around. I explained that I'm trying to qualify as the John Wanamaker of used books.

Her friend picked up a book on the pre-Raphaelites and gave us Daniel Gabriel Rosetti lamenting the wife to whom he was unfaithful, who died young of grief. Out of guilt and regret for his philandering Daniel buried her with the manuscript of his unpublished poems. He soon regretted the poems more than the wife, had them both exhumed and—poems only—published.

I showed her *The Best Letters of Thomas Jefferson* I'd brought along, told her how as president he'd let it be known that he'd be glad to receive and would answer letters from the public. He undertook to pay the postage both ways himself— an important thing when to send a single sheet might cost half of what a laborer earned in a day.

I read aloud a letter he wrote to James Madison about the debt on Monticello and how it weighed on him, his plan to conduct a land lottery to pay things down. It ends: *"But why afflict you with these details? Indeed, I cannot tell, unless pains are lessened by communication with a friend. The friendship which has subsisted between us, now half a century, and the harmony of our political principles and pursuits, have been sources of constant happiness to me through that long period."* (February 17, 1826)

I sold her that and Jefferson's *Garden Book*. It's a pleasure to sell, knowing the winter she'll have reading his planting and building notes, letters, musings (on Colonel Lewis in his decline, *"We can never lose a better man"*).

I took in $308 between 9:00 and 1:00.

Driving home it occurred to me that I'd keep a bar for the same reasons I do this: I like the smells of bourbon, Scotch, and beer separately and all mixed together with cigars, pipes, cigarettes, and talk, and I like helping myself to whatever appeals at the moment. I like lulls, paying myself by sampling my wares, shopping for myself from my own tables, buying all I want.

I've learned from Tom that people need to be *sold* books. It's a mistake to think that folks know what they want. Most readers are willing to have their susceptibility tried and even stretched a little. So we swell and puff like Falstaff to share enthusiasms and mind each other's business, or what's the passion for? Real booksellers at work glow like musicians when they're making music.

> *No, my good lord: banish Peto, banish Bardolph, banish Poins; but for sweet Jack Falstaff, kind Jack Falstaff, true Jack Falstaff, valiant Jack Falstaff, and therefore more valiant being, as he is, old Jack Falstaff, banish not him thy Harry's company, banish plump Jack, and banish all the world!*
>
> —Shakespeare, *King Henry IV, Part I*

AFTERWORD

As part of Thoreau's accounting, it mattered to him that he returned Ralph Waldo Emerson's ax sharper than when he borrowed it. I can't say I returned Zora in better shape than when we first went off together, but she was cleaner, looked spiffy with her three-tones simonized and her windows gleaming. I reinstalled all the amenities like seats and heat vents that Martha had stripped out to carry paintings, and I embellished it with a handsome side-view mirror that would do for an eighteen-wheeler. I blacked the tires with the stuff they use at used-car lots and rubbed the kickboards down with something to make them glossy and good-smelling.

But that first start on a cold day—if she starts at all—gives away a lot. I asked our mechanic what the chattering and smoke were all about. "Valves," he said darkly. He sold it for us "as is"—more appropriate for a car than for any book. Martha settled for all the cash the buyer could get on her credit card, just over $600. I felt guilty letting my machine go—a lady I'd slept with so often and ridden so hard—but I was cheered when Zora started right up for her new owner. The lady seemed not to notice the smoke, gave a brave wave as she roared off.

For a while now Martha has had her eye on a van the telephone company is giving up. It is as plain as its "Econoline" name, no windows on the side, no extras, just van. And engine—a V-8. At fourteen miles to the gallon it makes the Arabs smile. It will carry larger paintings and more books than the *ur* Zora, and its big, chalky white sides tempt me to muralize like Gulley Jimson. I want to paint scruffy books and leather

editions all the way around her Ford bulk, "Zora's Books" in
black letters across the slanting hood and broad rear doors. But
the van I dozed off dreaming about was Toad's in *The Wind in
the Willows*, his *"gipsy caravan, shining with newness, painted
a canary-yellow picked out with green, and red wheels."*

I did my taxes. It's a curious thing in *Walden* when Henry
gives his accounting. You wouldn't think anyone would care,
but he does it a couple of times, once when he buys a broken-
down shed for the nails and again when he figures his profit
on the beans he grew. It turns out that telling about money is
arresting. So here's mine: For the year, I sold and gave away
6300 books, beating Borrow's record and giving Vachel
Lindsay a run too. Counting in my expenses, I lost $1892 after
paying myself nothing and, marking down the books, I ended
the year with what I think I might actually get for them some-
day. There's water damage and mildew but no inflation in this
business. Weather, sun, the wear and tear of boxing, setting
out and re-boxing take their toll. I like it that accountants put
"(loss)" in parentheses, a little secret only to be whispered.

When I started my law practice the bankrupt petitioner had
to surrender everything to his creditors except two suits of
clothes (one for work, one for church), his Bible, some farm
tools, his cow, fifty pounds of flour, and a sack of seed grain.
Things are better now. My personal exemption will cover my
library and my computer as tools of the trade, plus a car or a
truck if I own one when I go down. Enough to go off with and
come in free. Kind of like Lewis & Clark.

The tall old Marine I met on the Fourth of July—the guy
who'd defended dropping the Bomb—turned out to be a
retired Macmillan editor. I pointed out some good Macmillan
books I had, a few he'd had a hand in publishing as it turned
out. He bought some of my groceries and praised my work. I
gave him a chapbook.

We talked as he moseyed. He asked me about the current fiction I carry (almost none), recommended Richard Powers, Ford Maddox Ford, and a novel about Henry VIII's time called *The Man on a Donkey* by Hilda Prescott. Then he asked if I'd ever heard of Clarence Day.

"No."

"*Life with Father*? You've arrived at this advanced state of adulthood and not heard of Clarence Day?"

"Uh-huh."

"And *you're* supposed to be doing the heavy lifting in this business! Well, he said some good things about books."

"What?"

"I was afraid you were going to ask me that. I can't quote it from memory."

I had a hunch he was holding back. "Do you have it on you?"

He did. He fumbled in his wallet, pulled out a shabby paper, smoothed it. He started to read. His voice got husky. He wiped his nose. "I can never get through this damn thing without choking up."

As it turned out, neither of us could:

> *The world of books is the most remarkable creation of man. Nothing else that he builds ever lasts. Monuments fall, nations perish, civilizations grow old and die out, and after an era of darkness new races build others. But in the world of books are volumes that have seen this happen again and again, and yet live on, still young, still as fresh as the day they were written, still telling men's hearts of the hearts of men centuries dead.*

> —Clarence Day
> *The Story of Yale University Press*

ZORA'S LIST

These are some of the authors and titles I like to carry. I haven't read them all. Many are here on hearsay. I buy them when I find them cheap enough, but on any given day only about a third are represented in my boxes. Many lucky discoveries among the riff-raff have made their way out of the rabble to the List, most recently Hans Zisser's Rats, Lice and History. *I now buy every copy I come upon. My gaping holes of ignorance and prejudice want mending. Send the names of your candidates to Zora, 126 Elm St., Hatfield, MA 01038.*

Abbey, Edward
Desert Solitare
Ackerley, A.J.K.
Letters
My Dog Tulip
Adams, Henry
The Education of Henry
Adams
Mont St. Michel and Chartres
Addison, Richard
Spectator Papers
Aesop
Fables
Agee, James, and Walker Evans
Let Us Now Praise
Famous Men
Aguecheek
My Unknown Chum
Aiken, Conrad
Poems
Ushant
essays, letters
Alcott, Louisa May
any title

Algren, Nelson
any title
Allingham, William
Diary
Alvarez, Alfred
any title
Amis, Kingsley
Lucky Jim
Ammons, A.R.
Poems
Andersen, Hans Christian
Fairy Tales
Anderson, Edgar
Plants, Man & Life
Anderson, Sherwood
Winesburg, Ohio
Apuleius
The Golden Ass
Arciniegas, Germàn
Amerigo and the New World
Arnold, Matthew
Poems
Aubrey, John
Brief Lives

Auchincloss, Louis
Love Without Wings
Auden, W.H.
any title
Aurelius, Marcus
Meditations
Austen, Jane
any title
Auster, Paul
any title
Austin, Mary
The Land of Little Rain

Bacon, Sir Francis
Essays
Bailey, Liberty Hyde
Hortus
Baldwin, James
any title
Balzac, Honoré de
any title
Baring, Maurice
Have You Anything to Declare?
Baring-Gould, William S.
The Annotated Mother Goose
Barker, George
Poems
Barth, John
The Floating Opera
Bartlett, John
Familiar Quotations
Bartram, William
Travels
Bashó, Matsuo
Poems
Bate, Walter Jackson
John Keats
Samuel Johnson
Baudelaire, Charles
Essays
The Flowers of Evil
Beckett, Samuel
any title

Behrman, S.N.
Duveen
People in a Diary
Belloc, Hilaire
The Path to Rome
Places
Bellow, Saul
any title
Benét, Steven Vincent
John Brown's Body
Western Star
Benét, William Rose
The Readers Companion
Benson, E.F.
any title
Berendt, John
*Midnight in the Garden
of Good and Evil*
Berger, John
Ways of Seeing
Bernanos, Georges
The Diary of a Country Priest
Berry, Wendell
Essays
Berryman, John
Poems
Beston, Henry
Herbs
Northern Farm
Outermost House
Betjaman, John
any title
Bettelheim, Bruno
The Uses of Enchantment
Bible (King James version)
Bishop, Elizabeth
Essays
One Art (Letters)
Poems
Stories
Blackburn, Paul
Poems
Blake, William
Poems

Bloom, Harold
  any title
Bly, Robert
  Essays
  Poems
Blyth, R.H.
  Haiku
Blythe, Robert
  Akenfield
Boccaccio, Giovanni
  The Decameron
Bogan, Louise
  any title
Boorstein, Daniel J.
  any title
Borges, Jorge Luis
  any title
Boswell, James
  any title
Bowen, Catherine Drinker
  any title
Bowles, Paul
  The Sheltering Sky
Brett, Simon, ed.
  The Faber Book of Diaries
Brewer
  Dictionary of Phrase and Fable
Bronowski, Jacob
  any title
Bronte, Charlotte
  any title
Bronte, Emily
  any title
Brooke, Rupert
  poems
Brooks, Van Wyck
  The Flowering of New England
  New England: Indian Summer
Brown, Rita Mae
  any title
Browne, Sir Thomas
  any title

Broyard, Anatole
  Kafka Was the Rage
Bruyère, Jean de la
  Characters
Buchan, John (First Baron
  Tweedsmuir)
  Pilgrim's Way
Bunyan, John
  The Pilgrim's Progress
Burgess, Anthony
  A Clockwork Orange
  Nothing Like the Sun
Burnett, Frances Hodgson
  A Little Princess
  The Secret Garden
Burns, Robert
  poems, letters
Burton, Richard
  The Arabian Nights
  Entertainments
Burton, Robert
  Anatomy of Melancholy
Butler, Samuel
  Notebooks
  The Way of the Flesh
Byatt, A.S.
  any title
Bynner, Witter
  The Chinese Translations
  poems, letters
Byrd, William
  The Secret Diary
Byron, George Gordon (Lord)
  poems, letters, journals
Byron, Robert
  The Road to Oxiana

Camus, Albert
  Notebooks
  The Stranger
  essays
Caesar, Julius
  The Gallic Wars

Cairns, Huntington, ed.
The Limits of Art
Campbell, Joseph
any title
Capote, Truman
any title
Carr, J.L.
any title
Carrighar, Sally
any title
Carroll, Lewis
Alice's Adventures in
Wonderland
Through the Looking Glass
Carruth, Hayden
poems, essays
Carson, Rachel
The Sea Around Us
Cary, Joyce
any title
Cather, Willa
any title
Catullus, Gais Valerius
poems
Cecil, David
any title
Celine, Louis-Ferdinand
any title
Cellini, Benvenuto
Memoirs/Autobiography
Cendrars, Blaise
any title
Ceram, C.W.
Gods, Graves and Scholars
Cervantes, Miguel de
Don Quixote
(Putnam translation and
Viking Portable edition)
Chartier, Émile ("Alain")
Essays
On Happiness
Chatwin, Bruce
any title
Chaucer, Geoffrey
The Canterbury Tales
(Viking Portable edition)

Chekhov, Anton
any title
Chesterfield, (Lord) Philip Dormer
Stanhope
Letters
Chesterton, Gilbert Keith
any title
Cicero, Marcus Tullius
any title
Cipolla, Carlo
Guns, Sails & Empires
Clark, Kenneth
any title
Clarke, Arthur
any title
Cleland, John
Fanny Hill, or Memoirs of
a Woman of Pleasure
Cocteau, Jean
any title
Coetzee, J.M.
Life & Times of Michael K
Coleridge, Samuel Taylor
poems, journals
Colette, Sidonie Gabrielle
any title
Columbia Encyclopedia (one
volume)
Connell, Evan S.
Mr. Bridge
Mrs. Bridge
Connolly, Cyril
any title
Conrad, Joseph
any title
Conway, Jill Kerr
The Road from Coorain
Cortázar, Julio
any title
Cowper, William
Letters
Cox, Kenyon
The Classical Point of View
Crane, Hart
Poems

Dumas, Alexandre
  The Count of Monte Cristo
  The Man in the Iron Mask
  The Three Musketeers
Duras, Marguerite
  The Lover
  The Malady of Death
  The Sea Wall
Durrell, Gerald
  My Family & Other Animals
Durrell, Lawrence
  any title

Eberhart, Richard
  poems
Eliot, Charles W.
  John Gilley
  (and any other titles in the True
    American Types series)
Eliot, George
  Daniel Deronda
  Middlemarch
  Romola
Eliot, T.S.
  any title
Ellison, Ralph
  The Invisible Man
Ellmann, Richard
  James Joyce
  Oscar Wilde
Emerson, Ralph Waldo
  Essays
  Journals
  Lectures
  Poems
    (Viking Portable edition)
Erickson, Eric
  any title
Evelyn, John
  Diary

Fabre, Jean Henri
  any title

Fairbrother, Nan
  The Cheerful Day
  An English Year
Farb, Peter
  Face of North America
Faulkner, William
  any title
Fermor, Patrick Leigh
  any title
Fielding, Henry
  Tom Jones
Finch, Robert, and John Elder, eds.
  *The Norton Book of Nature
    Writing*
Fisher, M.F.K.
  any title
Fitzgerald, F. Scott
  any title
Flanner, Janet
  any title
Flaubert, Gustav
  Madame Bovary
  Salambo
  Sentimental Education
Fletcher, Colin
  *The Man Who Walked
    Through Time*
Fontaine, Jean de la
  Fables
Ford, Ford Madox
  The Good Soldier
Forester, Cecil Scott
  Hornblower series
Forster, E.M.
  Howards End
  Maurice
  A Passage to India
  A Room with a View
  Where Angels Fear to Tread
Fowles, John
  any title
Frank, Anne
  The Diary of a Young Girl

Franklin, Benjamin
  Autobiography
  Papers (any and all volumes)
  Poor Richard's Almanac
Fraser, Lady Antonia
  any title
Frazer, George
  The Golden Bough
Freud, Sigmund
  any title
Frost, Robert
  Collected Poems
Fuentes, Carlos
  The Old Gringo
Fussell, Paul, ed.
  Class
  The Great War and
    Modern Memory
  The Norton Book of Travel

Gaddis, William
  The Recognitions
Galbraith, John Kenneth
  The Scotch
Gallico, Paul
  any title
Garrett, George
  any title
Gaskell, Elizabeth
  Cranford
Gass, William
  any title
Gay, Peter
  any title
Gibbon, Edward
  Autobiography
  The Decline and Fall of
    the Roman Empire
  English Journal
    (Viking Portable edition)
Gibbon, Stella
  Cold Comfort Farm
Gide, André
  any title

Gilbert, Lynn, and Gaylen Moore
  Particular Passions
Ginsberg, Allen
  poems
Gissing, George
  The Private Papers of
    Henry Ryecroft
Goethe, Johann Wolfgang von
  Faust
  Italian Journey
  The Sorrows of Young Werther
Gombrich, E.H.
  The Story of Art
Goodman, Paul
  Growing Up Absurd
Gould, Stephen Jay
  any title
Grahame, Kenneth
  Dream Days
  The Golden Age
  The Wind in the Willows
Graves, John
  From a Limestone Ledge
  Good-bye to a River
Graves, Robert
  Goodbye to All That
  Greek Anthology
  King Jesus
  The White Goddess
  poems, essays
Gray, Thomas
  poems
Greene, Graham
  any title
Grimm's Fairy Tales
Gunn, Thomas
  poems

Hakluyt, Richard
  Voyages
Hanff, Helene
  84, Charing Cross Road
  Q's Legacy
Hapgood, Fred
  Up the Infinite Corridor

Hardy, Thomas
  The Mayor of Casterbridge
  Tess of the D'Urbervilles
  poems, letters
Harris, Joel Chandler
  His Songs and His Sayings
  Uncle Remus
Hart-Davis, Rupert
  Letters
Hartley, Dorothy
  Lost Country Life
Harvard Classics
  Essays English and American
  Famous Prefaces
  Franklin, Woolman, Penn
Hawkes, Jaquetta
  A Land
Hay, John, and Peter Farb
  The Atlantic Shore
Hazlitt, William
  any title
Heaney, Seamus
  Poems
Heiser, Charles B.
  Of Plants and People
Heller, Joseph
  Catch-22
  Good as Gold
Henley, W.E.
  poems
Heraclitus
  On Nature
Herodotus
  The Histories
Herrick, Robert
  poems
Herriott, James
  All Creatures Great and Small
Hesiod
  Theogony
  Works and Days
Hesse, Hermann
  any title

Hillaby, John
  any title
Hine, Reginald
  Confessions of an
    Uncommon Attorney
Hoffer, Eric
  The True Believer
Holmes, Oliver Wendell
  The Autocrat of the
    Breakfast Table
  The Professor of the
    Breakfast Table
Holmes, Oliver Wendell, Jr.
  Letters
Homer
  The Iliad
  The Odyssey
  (Pope, Lattimore, or
    Fitzgerald, trans.)
Hopkins, Gerard Manley
  Poems
Horace
  Poems
Horgan, Paul
  Great River
  Lamy of Santa Fe
Houseman, A.E.
  any title
Hudson, W.H.
  any title
Hughes, Ted
  poems
Hugo, Victor
  any title
Huizinga, J.
  The Waning of the
    Middle Ages
Hurston, Zora Neale
  Their Eyes Were
    Watching God
Huxley, Aldous
  Brave New World

Irving, John
any title

Jackson, Holbrook
any title
James, Henry
any title
James, P.D.
any title
Jarrell, Randall
poems
Jeffers, Robinson
poems, letters
Jefferson, Thomas
Garden Book
Jewett, Sarah Orne
The Country of the Pointed Firs
Johnson, Samuel
any title
Jonson, Ben
any title
Joyce, James
any title
Jung, Carl Gustav
any title

Kafka, Franz
any title
Kakuzo, Okakura
Book of Tea
Kastner, Joseph
A Species of Eternity
Kawabata, Yasunari
Snow Country
Thousand Cranes
Kazin, Alfred
A Walker in the City
Keats, John
Letters
Poems
Kelly, Amy
Eleanor of Aquitaine
and the Four Kings
Kempis, Thomas à
Imitation of Christ

Kenner, Hugh
any title
Kermode, Frank
essays
Kesey, Ken
One Flew Over the Cuckoo's
Nest
Khayyam, Omar
Rubaiyat
Kilvert, Francis
Diary
Kincaid, Jamaica
any title
Kingston, Maxine Hong
The Woman Warrior
Kinnell, Galway
Walking Down the Stairs
poems
Kipling, Rudyard
any title
Kirkegaard, S.
any title
Kluger, Richard
Simple Justice
Krutch, Joseph Wood
any title
Kundera, Milan
any title
Kunitz, Stanley
poems

Larkin, Philip
any title
Lasch, Christopher
any title
Lawrence, D.H.
any title
Lawrence, T.E.
The Seven Pillars of
Wisdom
Leach, Bernard
A Pottery Book
Lear, Edward
any title

Leavis, F.R.
 any title
Lee, Laurie
 As I Walked Out One
  Midsummer Morning
 Cider with Rosie
Lees-Milne, James
 Diaries
Leighton, Ann
 Early American Gardens
Leopold, Aldo
 A Sand County Almanac
Lessing, Doris
 The Golden Notebook
Levering, Frank, and Wanda
 Urbanska
 Simple Living
Levi, Carlo
 Christ Stopped at Eboli
Lewis, C.S.
 any title
Liebling, S.J.
 Between Meals
Lindsay, Vachel
 Poems
Llewellyn, Richard
 How Green Was My Valley
London, Jack
 any title
Lopez, Claude-Anne
 Franklin and the Ladies of Paris
 Mon Cher Papa
 The Private Franklin
Lord, James
 Giacometti
Lorenz, Konrad
 An Aggression
 King Solomon's Ring
Lorenzini, Carlo ("C Collodi")
 Pinocchio
Lowell, Robert
 poems
Lowry, Malcolm
 Poems
 Under the Volcano

Lucretius
 On the Nature of the Universe

Macaulay, Rose
 Personal Pleasure
Macdonald, George
 Phantastes
Maclean, Fitzroy
 any title
Mailer, Norman
 The Naked and the Dead
Mallon, Thomas, ed.
 A Book of One's Own
Malraux, André
 Voices of Silence
Mann, Thomas
 any title
Mansfield, Katherine
 Letters
Marquez, Don
 Archy & Mehitabel
Marquez, Gabriel Garcia
 any title
Marvell, Andrew
 poems
Marx, Leo
 The Machine in the Garden
Masters, Edgar Lee
 Spoon River Anthology
Masters, Hilary
 Last Stands
Matthiessen, Peter
 any title
Mattingly, Garrett
 The Armada
Maupassant, Guy de
 any title
Maxwell, Gavin
 Ring of Bright Water
Maxwell, William
 any title
May, Rollo
 The Courage to Create
McCarthy, Mary
 any title

McCullers, Carson
  any title
McGrath, Thomas
  poems
McPhee, John
  any title
Mehta, Ved
  any title
Melville, Herman
  any title
Mendawar, Peter
  any title
Merrill, James
  any title
Merton, Thomas
  The Seven Story Mountain
Merwin, W.S.
  Unframed Originals
  poems, translations
Millay, Edna St. Vincent
  any title
Miller, Arthur
  any title
Miller, Henry
  any title
Milne, A.A.
  any title
Mintz, Sidney W.
  Sweetness and Power
Mitchell, Joseph
  McSorley's Wonderful Saloon
Mitford, Mary Russell
  Our Village
Moffat, Mary Jane, and Charlotte
Painter
  Revelations: Diaries of Women
Montagu, (Lady) Mary Wortley
  letters, journals
Montaigne, Michel de
  Essays
  Travel Journal
Moore, Marianne
  any title

Moorehead, Alan
  any title
Morley, Christopher
  The Haunted Bookshop
  John Mistletoe
  Parnassus on Wheels
  Shandygaff
Morris, Jan
  any title
Morris, Willie
  North Toward Home
Morris, Wright
  A Cloak of Light
  Will's Boy
Morrison, Samuel Eliot
  Christopher Columbus, Mariner
Morrison, Toni
  any title
Mortimer, John
  any title
Moss, Howard
  poems
Mother Goose
Mowat, Farley
  The Dog Who Wouldn't Be
  My Father's Son
  Never Cry Wolf
Muir, Edwin
  poems, essays
Munro, Alice
  Dance of the Happy Shades
Munthe, Axel
  The Story of San Michele
Murphy, Robert Cushman
  Logbook for Grace

Nabokov, Vladimir
  Ada, or Ardor
  Lolita
  Speak Memory
Naipaul, V.S.
  any title
Nash, Roderick
  Wilderness and the American
  Mind

Nearing, Helen, and Scott Nearing
  Living the Good Life
  The Maple Sugar Book
Neruda, Pablo
  Memoirs
  poems
Nichols, John
  Literary Anecdotes
  The Milagro Beanfield War
Nietzsche, Friedrich
  any title
Nin, Anaïs
  any title
Norwich, John Julius
  Christmas Crackers

O'Brian, Flann
  At Swim-Two-Birds
  The Third Policeman
O'Connor, Flannery
  Letters
O'Faolain, Sean
  Vive Moi!
Olson, Charles
  any title
Olson, Tillie
  I Stand Here, Ironing
Ondaatje, Michael
  any title
Origo, Iris
  any title
Orwell, George
  any title
Osborne, Dorothy
  Letters
O'Sullivan, Maurice
  Twenty Years A-Growing
Owen, Wilfred
  poems

Paglia, Camille
  Sex, Art, and American Culture
  Sexual Personae
Painter, George
  Proust

Paley, Grace
  any title
Panofsky, Erwin
  Studies in Iconology
Parkman, Francis
  any title
Pascal, Blaise
  Pensées
Pasternak, Boris
  Dr. Zhivago
  Safe Conduct
  poems
Pater, Walter
  Appreciations
  *The Renaissance: Studies
    in Art and Poetry*
Peattie, Donald Culross
  An Almanac for Moderns
  Green Laurels
Pepys, Samuel
  Diary (any and all volumes)
Percy, Walker
  any title
Perrault, Charles
  any title
Perrin, Noel
  A Reader's Delight
Petrarch, Francesco Petrarca
  any title
Phillips, Adam
  *On Kissing, Tickling and
    Being Bored*
Pissaro, Camille
  Letters to Lucien
Plath, Sylvia
  any title
Plato
  any title
Platt, Rutherford
  The Great American Forest
Plimpton, George, ed.
  Writers at Work (any volume)
Pliny
  The Natural History

Plomer, William
Autobiography
Plutarch
Lives
Polo, Marco
The Travels
Potter, Beatrix
any title
Pound, Ezra
The ABC of Reading
poems
Powers, Richard
any title
Prescott, H.F.M.
The Man on a Donkey
Prescott, Orville
History as Literature
Priestly, J.B.
any title
Pritchett, V.S.
any title
Proust, Marcel
any title (C.K. Moncrieff, trans.)
Pryor, Felix, ed.
The Faber Book of Letters
Pyle, Howard
Men of Iron
Otto of the Silver Hand
Robin Hood
Pym, Barbara
A Very Private Eye

Quennell, Peter
any title
Quiller-Couch, Arthur, ed.
The Oxford Book of English Prose
The Oxford Book of English Verse (1250–1918)

Rabelais, François
Gargantua and Pantagruel
(Urquart/Motteux trans.)
Ray, David
poems

Read, Conyers
The Tudors
Reid, Alaistair
Whereabouts
poems, essays
Renault, Mary
any title
Rexroth, Kenneth
poems, essays
Rhys, Jean
Smile Please
Rilke, Rainer Maria
Letters on Cezanne
Letters to a Young Poet
Poems
Rimbaud, Arthur
any title
Robinson, Edward Arlington
poems
Roethke, Theodore
Collected Poems
Ross, James Bruce, and Mary
Martin McLaughlin, eds.
The Renaissance Reader
Rostand, Edmond
Cyrano de Bergerac
(Brian Hooker trans.)
Roth, Henry
Call It Sleep
Roth, Philip
any title
Rousseau, Jean-Jacques
Confessions
Rowse, A.L.
any title
Ruskin, John
Modern Painters

Sackville-West, Vita
Garden Book
Sade, Marquis de
any title
Sagan, Carl
The Dragons of Eden

Salinger, J.D.
  any title
Sandburg, Carl
  any title
Santayana, George
  The Last Puritan
Saroyan, William
  any title
Sarton, May
  any title
Sauer, Carl Ortwin
  any title
Schaller, George B.
  any title
Schama, Simon
  any title
Scott, Paul
  The Raj Quartet
Schuster, M. Lincoln, ed.
  *A Treasury of the World's
    Great Letters*
Schwartz, Delmore
  Poems
Sendak, Maurice
  any title
Settle, Mary Lee
  any title
Sewell, Anna
  Black Beauty
Sexton, Anne
  poems
Shakespeare, William
  any title
Shapiro, Meyer
  Modern Art
Shaw, George Bernard
  Letters
Shikibu, Murasaki
  The Tale of Genji
Sitwell, Edith
  any title
Smith, Logan Pearsall
  A Treasury of English Prose
  Unforgotten Years

Smith, Stevie
  poems
Smith, Sydney
  Letters
Smollett, Tobias
  *The Expedition of
    Humphry Clinker*
  Peregrine Pickle
  Roderick Random
Snodgrass, W.D.
  poems
Snyder, Gary
  poems, essays
Sontag, Susan
  any title
Spence, Jonathan D.
  any title
Spender, Stephen
  any title
Stafford, Jean
  any title
Stanley, Arthur, ed.
  The Bedside Book
Steele, Richard, and Joseph
  Addison
  The Spectator
Stegner, Wallace
  Angle of Repose
  The Uneasy Chair
Stein, Gertrude
  *The Autobiography of
    Alice B. Toklas*
  Four Saints in Three Acts
Steinbeck, John
  East of Eden
  The Grapes of Wrath
  Letters
  The Sea of Cortez
  Travels with Charley
Steiner, George
  any title
Stendhal, Henri
  Charterhouse of Parma
  The Red and the Black

Sterne, Laurence
The Life and Opinions of
Tristram Shandy, Gentleman
A Sentimental Journey
Stevens, James
The Crock of Gold
Stevens, Wallace
any title
Stevenson, Robert Louis
any title
Strachey, Lytton
Eminent Victorians
Sutherland, James, ed.
The Oxford Book of English Talk
Suzuki, Shunryu
Zen Mind, Beginner's Mind
Swift, Jonathan
any title

Tanizaki, Junichiro
In Praise of Shadows
Taylor, Peter
any title
Tennyson, Alfred Lord
any title
Thackery, William Makepeace
Henry Esmond
Vanity Fair
Theroux, Alexander
The Primary Colors
Theroux, Paul
any title
Thesiger, Wilfred
Arabian Sands
Thomas, Dylan
any title
Thomas, Lewis
any title
Thompson, Flora
Lark Rise to Candleford
Thoreau, Henry David
any title
Thurber, James
Letters
The Thurber Carnival

Tolkien, J.R.R.
The Hobbit
The Lord of the Rings
Tolstoy, Leo
Anna Karenina
War and Peace
What Is Art?
What Men Live By
Tomlinson, Charles
any title
Toole, John Kennedy
A Confederacy of Dunces
Trollope, Anthony
any title
Trumbo, Dalton
Additional Dialogue (letters)
Tuchman, Barbara W.
any title
Turgenev, Ivan
any title
Twain, Mark
The Adventures of Tom Sawyer
Huckleberry Finn
The Innocents Abroad
Life on the Mississippi
Roughing It
The Tragedy of Puddinhead
Wilson

Updike, John
Essays

Valéry, Paul
any title
van der Post, Laurens
any title
Van Gogh, Vincent
letters
Vasari
Lives of the Artists
Veblen, Thorstein
The Theory of the Leisure Class
Verga, Giovanni
any title
Verlaine, Paul
any title

Virgil
  poems
Voltaire
  poems

Waddell, Helen
  any title
Waley, Arthur
  translations
Walker, Alice
  The Color Purple
Walpole, Horace
  Letters
Walton, Izaak
  The Compleat Angler
Warner, Sylvia Townsend
  Letters
Warner, William W.
  Beautiful Swimmers
Watts, Alan
  any title
Waugh, Evelyn
  letters
Weil, Simone
  Reader
Welty, Eudora
  any title
White, E.B
  Charlotte's Web
  Letters
  One Man's Meat
  The Points of My Compass
  The Second Tree from the Corner
  Stuart Little
  The Trumpet of the Swan
White, Gilbert
  A Natural History of Selborne
White, Patrick
  any title
White, T.H.
  England Have My Bones
  The Once and Future King
Whitman, Alden
  Come to Judgment

Whitman, Walt
  Leaves of Grass
  Specimen Days
Wiesel, Elie
  any title
Wilbur, Richard
  essays, poems
Wilde, Oscar
  essays
Wilder, Thornton
  any title
Willey, Basil
  The Eighteenth Century
    Background
  The Seventeenth Century
    Background
Williams, Charles
  All Hallows Eve
Williams, Oscar, ed.
  Immortal Poems
Williams, Tennessee
  any title
Williams, William Carlos
  any title
Wilson, Colin
  The Outsider
Wilson, Edmund
  any title
Wilson, Edward O.
  any title
Wolfe, Thomas
  any title
Wolfe, Tom
  essays
Wolff, Tobias
  This Boy's Life
Woolf, Leonard
  any title
Woolf, Virginia
  any title
Woollcott, Alexander
  essays
Wordsworth, Dorothy
  Journals

ABOUT THE AUTHOR

Because *Parnassus on Wheels* was read aloud to him as a boy, Alan Armstrong always imagined himself a Merchant Adventurer dealing in books. He started volunteering in a friend's bookshop—mostly walking the shop poodle—when he was eight. At fourteen he was selling books at the Brentano's outlet in his home town of Silver Spring, Maryland. Since then he has practiced environmental law in Philadelphia and been a partner in a small publishing company, Toll & Armstrong.

Armstrong graduated from Haverford College in 1961, got a degree in public policy from Princeton University, and, in 1966, received a J.D. degree from Yale University. He is married to the painter Martha Armstrong, and they live in Massachusetts. They have two children.

When the law business slows down, Armstrong loads up his wife's van with good used books and sets out to sell them wherever he finds a promising place. If your yard or parking lot is comely, let him know.

Wordsworth, William
  poems
Wright, Esmond
  Franklin of Philadelphia
Wright, Richard
  any title
Wylie, Elinor
  poems
Wyss, J.R.
  The Swiss Family Robinson

Yeats, William Butler
  any title
Yevtushenko, Yevgeny
  poems
Yourcenar, Marguerite
  Memoirs of Hadrian
Yutang, Lin
  The Importance of Living

Zisser, Hans
  Rats, Lice and History
Zukofsky, Louis
  Prepositions

General Wants:
  Library of America titles
  Oxford Book of . . . series
  Most Modern Library titles
  Most Penguin titles
  Any Viking Portable
  Best American Essays . . . series
  Best American Short
    Stories . . . series
  Almost any poetry anthology
  Almost any atlas
  Almost any dictionary